STOLEN LIGHT

STEWART CONN

Stolen Light

SELECTED POEMS

BLOODAXE BOOKS

ISBN: 1 85224 484 4

First published 1999 by
Bloodaxe Books Ltd,
P.O. Box 1SN,
Newcastle upon Tyne NE99 1SN.

Bloodaxe Books Ltd acknowledges
the financial assistance of Northern Arts.

Cover printing by J. Thomson Colour Printers Ltd, Glasgow.

Printed in Great Britain by
Cromwell Press Ltd, Trowbridge, Wiltshire.

For Judy

Acknowledgements

The poems in this selection are drawn primarily from *Thunder in the Air* (Akros Publications, Preston, 1967); *Stoats in the Sunlight* (1968), *An Ear to the Ground* (1972) and *Under the Ice* (1978), all Hutchinson, London; *In the Kibble Palace* (1987), *The Luncheon of the Boating Party* (1992) and *In the Blood* (1995), all Bloodaxe Books, Newcastle upon Tyne; and *At the Aviary* (Snailpress, Cape Town, 1995). Grateful acknowledgement is made to all these publishers.

For permission to include previously uncollected poems I am grateful to the editors of *After the Watergaw* (Scottish Cultural Press, 1998), *Carapace, Fabrique* (France), *The Herald*, *Janus* (USA), *New Writing Scotland* (ASLS, 1997), *Present Poets* (National Museums of Scotland, 1998), *The Scotsman*, *Skinklin Star* and *Workshop New Poetry*; and to BBC Radio Scotland and Radio 3.

While the poems are grouped thematically rather than strictly conforming with the volumes in which they first appeared, their original chronology is in the main preserved.

Contents

VII

I

Todd

My father's white uncle became
    arthritic and testamental in
    lyrical stages. He held cardinal sin
was misuse of horses, then any game

won on the sabbath. A Clydesdale
    to him was not bells and sugar or declension
    from paddock, but primal extension
of rock and soil. Thundered nail

turned to sacred bolt. And each night
    in the stable he would slaver and slave
    at cracked hooves, or else save
bowls of porridge for just the right

beast. I remember I lied
    to him once, about oats: then I felt
    the brand of his loving tongue, the belt
of his own horsey breath. But he died,

when the mechanised tractor came to pass.
    Now I think of him neighing to some saint
    in a simple heaven or, beyond complaint,
leaning across a fence and munching grass.

Ferret

More vicious than stoat or weasel
because caged, kept hungry, the ferrets
were let out only for the kill:
an alternative to sulphur and nets.

Once one, badly mauled, hid
behind a treacle-barrel in the shed.
Throwing me back, Matthew slid
the door shut. From outside

the window, I watched. He stood
holding an axe, with no gloves.
Then it sprang; and his sleeves
were drenched in blood

where the teeth had sunk. I hear
its high-pitched squeal,
the clamp of its neat steel
jaws. And I remember

how the axe flashed, severing
the ferret's head,
and how its body kept battering
the barrels, long after it was dead.

Farm

The sun drills the shire through and through
till the farm is a furnace, the yard
a quivering wickerwork of flame. Pitchforks
rise and fall, bales are fiery ingots.
Straws sputter like squibs. Stones
explode. From the byre, smack on time,
old Martha comes clattering out
with buttered bannocks and milk in a pail.

Todd, his face ablaze, swims back
in what shadow there is. Hugh and John
stretch out among sheaves. Hens squabble
for crusts; a dog flicks its tail
at a cleg; blueflies bunch like grapes.
Still the sun beats down, a hammer
on tin. And high overhead vapour-trails
drift seaward, out past Ailsa Craig.

Harelaw

Ploughlands roll where limekilms lay
  seeping in craters. Where once dense
  fibres oozed against gatepost and fence
till staples burst, firm wheatfields sway;
  and where quarries reeked, intense

with honeysuckle, a truck dumps load
  upon load of earth, of ash and slag
  for the raking. Spliced hawsers drag
roots out and wrench the rabbit wood
  apart as though some cuckoo fugue

had rioted. On this mossy slope
  that raindrops used to drill and drum
  through dusk, no nightjar flits nor numb
hawk hangs as listening foxes lope
  and prowl; no lilac shadows thumb

the heavy air. This holt was mine
  to siege and plunder, here I caged
  rare beasts or swayed royally on the aged
backs of horses – here hacked my secret sign,
  strode, wallowed, ferreted, rampaged.

But acres crumple and the farm's new image
  spreads over the old. As I face
  its change, a truck tips litter; hens assess
bright tins, then peck and squawk their rage.
  The truck spurts flame and I have no redress.

Country Dance

Before the advent of the combine
the big mill would lumber from farm
to farm, spouting steam and flame:
stooks extending to the horizon
and beyond, weathered by sun or rain.

Intricate as a dance, was the tying
of the sheaves, on the ground
or against one thigh, to a communal
rhythm; then their hoisting
in the stackyard, forks flashing;

and as though riding on air,
the man on top, under steady
bombardment, circling and weaving,
gold ramparts rising round him
to a music compelling as any eightsome.

Ayrshire Farm

Every new year's morning the farmers
would meet at Harelaw with their guns
for the shoot. Mungo red in the face,
Matthew hale as a tree, John huge
in old leather. The others in dribs
and drabs, shotguns over their shoulders,
bags flopping at their sides, collars up.

We'd set out across the north park,
the glaur on our leggings freezing
as we left the shelter of the knowes.
No dogs. Even the ferrets on this day
of days left squealing behind
their wire. We'd fan out, taking
the slope at a steady tramp.

II

For three days and nights the stallion
lay shivering in its stall. Two nights
running, Todd stayed in the stable

mopping the fever up, packing blankets
and straw, trying a mixture of bran
and mash, all other tricks failing.

The beams stretched and shrank. The lamp
hissed. Next morning the byremen brought
ropes, and hauled. The dead weight slumped.

Nothing could get it to its feet. The breath
rotten, the flanks acid, its hindquarters
done. The vet came, in a yellow coat.

As he reached the door the stallion
came shuddering upright, head forking, eyes
huge and rolling, hooves flint on stone.

When it had been put down, Todd undid
his leggings, coughing up green rheum, asking why
each time the vet came a good beast had to die.

III

The yard is littered with scrap, with axles
and tyres, buckled hoops and springs – all rusting.
The wreckage of cars that have been dumped.

The hut is still there. In the doorway
two men talk horses – but not as he did
in the days when the Clydesdales came

to be shod, the milk-wagons for repair.
The din of iron on iron brings it all back:
Rob beating the anvil, to a blue flame;

the beast straining, the bit biting in,
horn burning, the sour tang of iron,
the sizzling, the perfect fit of the shoe.

In his mind's eye, the whole yard is teeming
with horses, ducking blackthorn, tails
swishing, the gates behind them clanging...

The men have started to strip an old van.
In passing he takes a kick at the wing. No one
notices. The dead metal does not ring at all.

IV

He draws horizons in, as the lark its area
of song. Now the singing is done. He lies
crookedly, his head on a coarse pillow,

the sheets held by a framework of wood.
It is as though he were already boxed in.
Now and then he pecks at a little food

or jitters his wrist against the beaker
I hold. One by one they visit him,
to dab his damp forehead with gauze.

At night they take the flowers to the hall,
but the sweet smell stays. As time draws
to a close, his eyes grow large. The flesh

is parchment, sticking to bone. His hands
shred the sheet. His gums clack. Small
sounds, like birds' beaks, pecking...

I want the sunlight to come shrieking in:
to send the soul soaring with song. All
I can do is turn and tiptoe from the room.

V

How he would stroke their muzzles, haul their brute
heads back, drive and pinion them against
the stable wall, throw round them bright chains.

Then bring armfuls of hay, water slopping
from buckets, oats stirred in a tub. Their breath
pounding round him, like bursts of steam.

22

One shoulder bent; his hands covered with sores,
with hacks and blisters, the marks of horses.
Still he combed them, pared hooves, dried the rank

sweat up. For whose sake he was lamed, gave up
meat and drink, lost sleep; with no thought
for the swifts in the eaves, the clegs pricking

the blood, the rats in the straw. I still see him
come cantering out to the yard, his brown serge
suit streaming, the horses under him neighing

and neighing. No more than half real. At once
fabulous and absurd. Like Goya, who went painting
at night with candles round the rim of his hat.

Stoats in the Sunlight

I once came across a pack of stoats in the sunlight,
    their eyes like jewels, the tips of their tails black.

One kept swinging on a fencepost and springing
    to the ground, leaving the wires twanging.

As at a word of command, they took up
    close formation and moved off in one direction.

Knowing what I do now, I wouldn't have stood there
    watching, imagining them such dainty playthings.

The Shed

When the milking was done, the byre
mucked out, and the cows bedded
for the night, I would creep to the shed
where the billy-goat was tethered

behind the bales. His hooves danced
as we fought, striking sparks
as I swung him by the scruff or had him
by the beard, butting and kicking.

Now and then a whinny, as he shook himself
free. His skull brick-hard, the eyes
twists of straw. Or I'd force cow-cake
on him: his stench filling the shed.

The farm has changed hands twice.
Last week I visited it, the first
time in years. As I passed the shed
a chain clanged – and I leapt aside

suddenly terrified that the goat
(or his wrinkled ghost) might come
slithering over the straw-bales,
pinning me back with his yellow eye.

Forebears

My father's uncle was the fastest
thing on two wheels, sitting in a gig,
the reins tight, his back at an angle
of thirty degrees, puffing up dust-clouds
as he careered down Craigie Hill.

His father before him, the strongest man
in Ayrshire, took a pair of cartwheels
by the axle and walked off with them: I have
visions of him in the meadow, holding
two ropes, a stallion straining on each.

Before that, no doubt, we boasted
the straightest furrow, the richest yield.
No measurements needed: each farm
bore its best, as each tree its fruit.
We even had a crazy creature in crinolines

who locked her letters in a brass box.
Others too ... but what do such truths
add up to – when the nearest
(and furthest) I get is visiting
their elaborately cared-for graves?

On an adjoining stone are a skull
and hourglass, from Covenanter
days. Their lives a duller
sacrifice. John on his moral staff,
the great-aunts with their rigid ways,

smacking of goodness in the strictest
sense, members of a sect, Elect almost,
shared surely something of flint
in the brain: their mortal goal
salvation, through purification of the soul.

On Craigie Hill

The farmhouse seems centuries ago,
the steadings slouched under a sifting of snow
for weeks on end, lamps hissing, logs stacked
like drums in the shed, the ice having to be cracked
to let the shaggy cats drink. Or
back from the mart through steaming pastures

men would come riding – their best
boots gleaming, rough tweeds pressed
to a knife-edge, pockets stuffed with notes.

Before that even, I could visualise (from coloured
prints) traps rattling, wheels spinning; furred
figures posing like sepia dolls
in a waxen world of weddings and funerals.
When Todd died, last of the old stagers,
friends of seventy years followed the hearse.
Soon the farm went out of the family: the Cochranes
going to earth or like their cousins
deciding it was time to hit town.

The last link broken, the farm-buildings stand
in a clutter below the quarry. The land
retains its richness – but in other hands.
Kilmarnock has encroached. It is hard to look
back with any sense of belonging.
Too much has changed, is still changing.
This blustery afternoon on Craigie Hill
I regard remotely the muddy track
my father used to trudge along, to school.

Craggy Country

Tales of Craigie Hill occupy my memory:
how at Mungo Farquhar's corner a pony
and trap, come recklessly adrift, sent driver
and passenger plummeting; the crazed beast,
flecked with foam, finally caught and quietened
outside the creamery, at Riccarton road-end.

I would think of this, as among empty churns
or clinging to the tailgate, I ascended
through morning mist to the farm: those
earlier generations like speeded-up figures
in Chaplin films, the frame frozen on Sundays,
men's boots gleaming, women in black lace.

Later on my second-hand Raleigh racer
with drop handle-bars I'd zigzag uphill,
squirming on the narrow saddle; on the return
journey imagining I was the first Scot
ever to win the Tour de France. Once,
eager to catch the cricket at Kirkstyle,

I cut things too fine and leaving my machine
described an arc in mid-air, in slow motion,
before landing; then headed painfully home
with the crumpled wheels and buckled frame
all grass and mud – object of derision
as townie come a cropper, or country buffoon.

Family Tree

In faded photographs, vanished generations
display shovel beards and gold watch-chains.
Here and there a sheepish smile, but in the main
they confront the future with old-fashioned
steadfastness of gaze. Flanked by cousins, austere
in their Sunday best, stands my great-uncle.

Churchill to him a warmonger, Stalin the Red Dragon
of the Apocalypse, he'd recite chapter and verse,
the Big Bible on his knee. On receiving the Gift
of Utterance from the Holy Ghost, he and his sisters
burst in on my father, studying for the ministry:
the World would end at noon next day: would he climb

Craigie Hill with them, to pray. They succeeded, unaided,
in keeping the Last Trump at bay. Thereafter
going into retreat – Martha 'staying with friends'
for a spell; the matter unlikely to have been
spoken of again, had not Todd on his death-bed
complained of '... live coals in the brain'.

Farm Funeral

His hearse should have been drawn by horses.
That's what he envisaged: the strain
and clop of crupper and chain, flashing
brass, fetlocks forcing high. With below
him, the frayed sheets turning slowly yellow.

On the sideboard a silver cup he had won,
inscribed 'to Todd Cochrane', now a lamp;
and tinted prints of his trotting days,
switch in hand, jockey-capped, the gig silky
with light, wheels exquisitely spinning.

For fifty years he was a breeder of horses;
nursing them nightly, mulling soft praise
long after the vet would have driven his plunger in.
Yet through them was his hip split. Twice
he was crushed by a stallion rearing.

Himself to the end unbroken. God's tool, yes,
that to earth will return. But not before time.
He ought to have been conveyed to the grave
by clattering Clydesdales, not cut off
from lark and sorrel by unseemly glass.

The shire is sprinkled with his ashes.
The fields are green through his kind. Their clay,
his marrow. As much as the roisterer, he: even
that last ride to Craigie, boots tightly laced,
his tie held in place by a diamond pin.

II

Afternoon

I lying on lichen can see
rivulets glancing in the sun
like fishes' scales or silver
sixpences. I rise and run

downhill until I reach a pool
wedged innocently between
two rocks, where lazy lizards slide
as if afraid of being seen

by heron or tell-tale poet. Then
a tasselled waterfall
that holds its breath only to spill
spindrift my thoughts. Suddenly all

grows quiet, as if today
as fossil has been overlapped
by some tomorrow only five
senses away but not yet mapped.

Thunder in the Air

On an evening fuzzy with heat
    and steeped in honey, I tear
through bracken: the threat
    of thunder hangs on stillest air.

Cows slump in pastures, crop
    pale clover, are yapped at
by threadbare dogs. Ponies droop
    across gateposts for the night.

The lark in upper reaches slips
    through song too pure to formalise,
unhinges dizzily, and flypes
    back to its dewy cage of grass.

Grey smirr of squirrel
    disappears up a pine tree -
stays in the abstract till
    showers of gold-dust give it away.

A breathless light bristles
    down branches, probes fur
from ferns. There is
    no need for disguises here,

and no need to reveal
    the beauty of this place.
I lift my head, and feel
    the huge rain slurping on my face.

Under Creag Mhor

A lizard fidgets in the sun
    that stuns it. Inchlong
    and perfect, agile among
pebbles, it purls its reflection

in crinkling pools. Neither
    freak nor fossil but something
    of each, legends clang
in its speck of a brain, roar

it down at no notice through brown
    peat juice, through mire
    of yellow bogland to where
it discovers its origin.

The bracken scurrs of Creag Mhor,
    pleated with clear water,
    no longer house dinosaur
and plated myth. But far

down, in the cool bright
    element of lizard's tiny
    being, in its ancient eye,
such monsters huddle yet.

In a Simple Light

Winter in this place
is a tangerine sun.
Against the skyline
nine Shetland ponies

stand like cut-outs
fraying at the edges.
Snow puffs and flurries
in weightless driblets

as they platter downhill,
pink-hooved, chins
stitched with frost, manes
jiggling a tinsel trail.

They clutter and jolt,
are pluff-bellied, biff
posts, thrum their trough
with warm breathing, smelt

ice. On the skyline
again, part fancy, they
freeze. In each eye
is a tangerine sun...

Setting

Strathglass, a confusion
    of colour. Broom and gorse
are transfiguration
    of yellow and gold. Furze

flames, myrtle steeps, is
    its singing fragrance. In
dusty silences, bees
    are pelted with pollen.

A breathless light
    thins and dribbles,
and haloes a mountain-goat
    maddened by midges. He nimbles

uphill, but falters as
    his shadow crops mine.
Poised, he sees
    me as shambling clown

invading his own.
    Then, gaelic mandarin,
he stilts over the sun.
    My gauze shadow is gone.

Margins

It is one thing to talk of terror
in the abstract, quite another
to face up to the particular,
fencing in a feeling of fear.

To speak say, of a mother
whose breast is touched by tumour;
or the less explicit horror
of a brother's mental disorder.

And most of all, in a rare
moment, to explain to a daughter
what margins are; the nature
of the charmed lives we bear.

The Chinese Tower

I

Hard land and dry, yet already
the lavender-clumps are bristling
like hassocks for Provençal ladies.

Crickets cross and uncross their legs.
The pine-slopes are musty. Soon
the valley will turn as on a spit.

In this world of bells, of goats
heavily thonged, thyme tracking
the tree-line, so single-minded

do the senses become that for them
the only escape is trussed brutally
to the bellies of great beasts.

II

But under rain, the land
is tin. There is brimstone
among the mountains.

Watertroughs overflow
like basins of wine.
Lightning fills the street.

Then two men with umbrellas
and between them
fifty sheep whose bells

are the din of a drowned
city. Now they are gone.
The crickets, too, are silent.

III

In as never before such blueness
(though to them the merest
translation of summer) two huntsmen

traverse the valley. They tack
as one, as yachts evenly paced;
though here in no breeze, but welter

of blueness. Even time can be treated
in terms of colour: nor arises
matter of identity. The cricket's

disguise, the butterfly fired
from slate – these are proof,
and part, of the same. You doubt it?

Watch then those huntsmen
scouring that hill. Watch them
halt, as one. Watch an arm

rise, and fall. And wait,
the length of the valley away,
for the sound of rushing stone.

IV

Or I find you, in a straw hat,
chasing butterflies. Even they
stress the oneness of it all

whose every movement is irretrievable
yet infinitely repeated. Such
is the truth not of this place only

but of things – hence of things
in this place. A bluetail shimmers
in a specific, no mere casual sun.

V

The waters of a mountain stream
assume the shape of ravine, then
create ravines of their own

in air. This in accordance
with the natural freedom
of things. And the village pump

always runs, a silver thread.
Ravine and rich chasm in one,
its surface is a source of light.

VI

High among pines, on a hill
overlooking the chapel, is a Chinese
tower. In both name, and style.

Behind it a viper lies coiled.
Is he lord of this place?
Has he an enquiring mind?

But the pines change from green
to smoky blue. Already there is
a chill in the air. Questions

need no answer. In absence
the presence of snake grows
strangely stronger. This square

of stone: an outlook tower.
Yet from few places can it be seen.
Certainly from nowhere in the village.

VII

Of the tower three things
are commonly said. That
at its base is a well

of pure water (this being
open to proof). That formerly
a tunnel led underground

to the village (this
to be taken on trust).
And thirdly that once,

in time of fire, monks
went dripping like candle-wax
down the face of the rock.

VIII

From the Chinese tower can be seen
the swerve of the valley, the lavender
fields and the mountains, pink

beyond. With finger in air
you can trace the tracks
of ravines, mark the pantiled roofs

of houses, of lofts, of the church
that strikes every hour twice.
And slowly, the blueness becomes

penetrable. There must always
be just such a place – its
tiny bells chinking in the wind.

[Thorame, Provence]

Old Actor

Not the same nowadays. They don't play
Shakespeare properly – not the way
we used to. Too superior
for a frontcloth, that's their

trouble. Opera use it, why not Theatre?
I mean, take the first scene from *Caesar* –
that ought to be played out front, the main
area set for the procession.

As for *Hamlet*, a gravedigger here
or there hardly matters any more.
(I saw Benson, as the Prince,
carried off after 'The rest is silence' –

but that *improved* the text.) Donat,
Martin-Harvey... what *style*. Another thing,
we'd always an orchestra in the pit
for the Bard – no loudspeaker in the wings.

Stage effects too: real waterfalls,
you name it – even Skegness,
still the gas floats. All they want these
days in a lad is, well you know ... *balls*.

Not that I'm against manliness,
anything of the sort. Bawdry for that matter.
I just think there are other
things that count, *besides* filling a codpiece.

North Uist

I

My new waders are like far-off dogs, whining.
My shoulder-strap could be a wheatear
turning a corner. The wind, through the cleat
of my landing-net, makes the squeaking
of many mice busying themselves under cover.
On his ledge overlooking the loch
the buzzard that is too big for a buzzard
eyes everything stonily, then takes his pick.

II

Uist, a smashed mirror.
I holiday here, to gather
strength for the winter.
So I fire my peats, gut
trout, rub cold hands together:
reassured that when December
does come, I shall be far
from here. Like all city dwellers.

III

I try to locate a tiny ratchet
at my right ear, an insomniac
cheese-grater somewhere beyond my toes.
The place is hoaching with mice. They are in
for the winter. Every so often
we have an eyeball to eyeball confrontation.
One way to dispose of them is to fire
the thatch. A costly operation.

IV

Three days I have trudged
after a pair of eagles; sighting them
occasionally, overhead or on fence-stakes,
surveying their land. This evening,

probing gobbets of fur, disgorged bone,
I am perceived by a hind who stands
sniffing, then bounds over the wire
and effortlessly away.

V

Striding back from the Co-op, I clutch
sodden groceries in a plastic bag
one handle of which is sprung.
Proud of the buffeting
I'm taking, I feel I belong:
till I meet a chained mongrel,
yap-yapping; and an old woman
who slurches past, head down.

VI

The sky consists of strips
of blue, like a holiday postcard.
I sit writing, like a man writing
a holiday postcard. The strips
turn to steel, to smoky grey.
The tide recedes, and recedes,
all the way to Vallay. Meanwhile
the multitudinous sandworms turn and turn.

VII

If, as the pundits say,
a new Ice Age does
come, well I suppose Uist
will be as ready as most.
The skuas sharp as razors;
the lochans, crystal.
And in the long chambers,
the War Lords are sleeping still.

Driving Through Sutherland

Here too the crofts were burned
to the ground, families stripped
and driven like cattle to the shore.
You can still hear the cursing,
the women shrieking.

                    The Duke
and his lady sipped port, had
wax in their ears. Thatch
blazed. Thistles were torn up
by the root.

          There are men
in Parliament today could
be doing more.

                    With these thoughts
in mind we drive from Overscaig
to Lairg, through a night as blue
as steel.

          Leaving Loch Shin behind
we find facing us an even colder
firth, and a new moon rising
delicately over a stubble field.

Summer, Assynt

(for John and Lynne Arnott)

Drumbeg

After three weeks' rain, Drumbeg is a swampland;
Suilven's tonsured skull lost
in mist. The forecasters extend
a blessing everywhere except 'the north-west'.

Marooned cattle peer
through columns of moisture.
The lochs are less Landseer
than Japanese watercolour.

By evening, we can see
the nearer hills. Under pale skies
summer visitors emerge – like empty
vessels, shifting in the breeze.

River Kircaig

Dear Lord Vestey
he had to write, *please*
accept my apologies
for fishing your water
with worm: otherwise
the ban would remain.
This after the discovery
of two cock salmon
along with his bait tin.
He gazes at anglers
in green chest-waders
casting monotonously.
Suddenly his expression
changes. Light glances
in his eyes as he sees,
through the birches,
two boys stealthily
pursuing old ways ...

Lochans

You, Loch Torr nan Hidhean
in the lee of Canisp, took some persuasion.
Loch a Braighe, you too showed a firm will
before yielding a speckled fighter from your cross-ripple.

Despite your chill, Loch Gorm Mor,
a change of fly finally got your measure.
Then on the way home
to fail with you, Lochan-of-no-Name:

naive enough to try
and outreach your pads of water-lily
I left in your dark bed an imprint deeper
than I care to remember.

Departure

'Leave the cooker and kitchen
as you find them: clean.'
On our last afternoon, as is proper,
we eliminate any reminder

of our presence – so that whoever
should be next here
finds no cup-ring or soup-stain
but all spick and span.

As for the land around, little need
for circumspection. A neap tide
laps where we clambered
or sat pullovered –

while long before we drive away
we will trickle into anonymity;
the wader-prints round each lochan
fished, by brimming waters filled in.

The Fox in His Lair

The fox in his lair
by oak-root and whorl
is presence, not scent
of fox. Is cold fury
of fur – soft pad
of cunning by night.

The badger in his burrow
no fairy-tale brock,
but paw crooked like a nut
ready to tear
the earth's skin
to get at the bone.

The raven, sweeping
in air, no line
on a blue plate; but
gorger of carrion, meat
in its gullet, slivers
trailing from each talon.

And you, my sweet,
how can you hope
to convince me
you are all sweetness –
when I know where
your hands have burrowed?

Like badger, like raven
and fox, who inhabit
domains of their own
in air, you are
no mere colour or scent
but of the earth, your rotten lair.

The Villagers

They will take over the village.
For them, we shall fashion
arrowheads, hammers from flint,
axes from the deer's horn.
They will have us build turf
walls, a fort every two miles.

Grain will be sown again, milk
skimmed of its cream. Copper
and tin mixed. We will spread
dung on the fields. Our women-folk
will teach them basket-work, how
to stretch boats from hide.

They will study our methods
of hooking fish, of trampling
black berries for wine. Before
each ceremony, they will watch
as we take a cockerel and slit
its throat over a tin basin.

When we have carved for them
gods of stone, and set them
on the mountain where our own
once were, that will be enough.
They will sharpen their knives,
and use our skin for drums.

Flight

Leaving the town behind, and the spoiled
    fields, we made slowly for the hills.
        Our clothes were in rags, our
        bodies lit with sores. Every
so often we had to water the horse.
Our farm-cart was heaped with straw. Under
        that, the real cargo.
        The soldiers scoffed. After
searching us, though, they let us through.

We dared not stop or look round.
    But from the side of the cart
        came a steady trickle of blood,
where the most drunken of the guards
    had run his sword in among the straw.

Vanities

I

Four knights are stationed at the Fountain
 of Tears, the first day of each month:
 where resides an effigy supporting a unicorn.

They pledge themselves
 to combat of arms: no lady may pass
 unless she give a gage, without a knight
breaking a lance for her in sport.

A medieval game of forfeits.

II

The blessed Philippe, improving
on Francis of Assisi, ordered

that he be laid in a sack,
an iron chain about his neck

and so placed to die. Then
to be buried naked at the entrance

to the choir, that everyone
might walk over his body, even goats

and dogs. This taking the place
of worldly vanity. *A fine treasure*

for worms.

III

The knight in silver,
 his lady in fur and miniver,
  dance the one dance.

Soon they will be lines
 carved on stone.

 I forget the king's name.

Omens and Disturbances

The gull

A gull lights on Troy. In all its travels
it has seen nothing like this. The beach
is stained. In the crevices
of the rocks are nests of fire.

Two armies trumpet on the plain, stopping
now and again to check on the rules.
The Greeks disembowel a goat, smearing
their faces with hot entrails.

Or gifts are exchanged: a shield,
a studded belt. Then the spears
curve, the helmets flash in the sun.
An axe rises and falls. Ajax

spills men's brains. Every so often
voices are heard from heaven. The bird
circles, out of reach of the smoke.
Suddenly it plummets, a white thunderbolt.

Helen

The noise and disorder distract me
from my tapestry. It is hot work,
albeit the point of my needle
is sharp. See, this done already:
the purple here is Greece; that pale
green, Troy – held on a single thread.

For weeks now the light has been bad,
a murky orange. I wish they would
settle things, out there. Still,
with my spices and pomegranates, I am
moderately contented. Besides, I find
one man's belly very much like another.

To Anchises

A few pots, a tinder trail. All that is left
of Troy. Where are its towers, its boudoirs now?
Hector's skull has been gutted, Priam struck
from behind by those bastards of Greeks.

To reach here I had to wade through gouts
of blood. Ye gods, Paris will have something
to answer for. That's it, up on my back.
Truly, this is a fine game we are playing.

The beggar

Let the beggar bend the bow, if he can.
His hair and beard are filthy. Such
a stinkard will not make fools of us.

He can hardly see the axes, never mind
make out the rings. Old enough to be her father,
and cracked besides. It is Telemachos

who tries our patience. Not that way,
dolt, or you break an arm. Once more:
after supper we shall find other amusement.

III

At Coruisk

I

Think of it: a honeymoon at the foot
of the Cuillin, and not once to see them
for mist – till on the last day we broached
from Elgol the seven crowned kings.

So intense the experience: not summer only,
but years, cramming one afternoon –
thus keenly the glimpse awaited.
Nor had been envisaged such blueness:

ice-crests mirrored in Coruisk, blue
upon blue, as we followed
the path home. The moon crescent.
The sky, powdered flint.

II

Tempting to see these things
as manifestations of the mind
significant through ourselves,
which precede and succeed our notice.

For all that, those shadows are real.
They darken or illumine, at will;
are points from which
to examine ourselves. But watch

how you go: yonder are scurrs
would cut you down; nearer
to hand, peat-holes
where you'd cramp and drown.

III

So we get to know landscape,
and each other, better;
our breathing filling the air
with each lap tackled. We learn

that the end of a road is seldom
a fixed point; bridges exist
too narrow to be crossed
more than one abreast.

And remains the fear, when
we look round, that two figures
not dissimilar to ourselves should appear
transparent, then vanish altogether.

Marriage a Mountain Ridge

I

Like most, one way or another, ours
has been through some dark couloirs.

I cannot swear to actual crevasses –
but have sensed them underfoot. (One night

on Bheinn Fhada I lost my footing,
and was fortunate a rowan took my weight.)

That way I am better equipped
for keeping, if not to the spirit, the letter.

Crampons and pitons fitted, we face
the next assault, roped together. I also carry

an ice-pick – but fear to use it,
lest it sink too deeply in.

II

Perhaps the hardest lesson
is to accept the Brocken,

the Man with the Rainbow, as stemming
from myself; a projection

of my own form. The cauldron
below me, thin air.

In these rarified labyrinths
the way forward

is to focus
on a fixed point,

one hand firmly gripping
its moral thread.

III
Whether scaling Etive
of the shifting faces

or on the summit of Blaven,
sheet-ice glistening

through walls of mist,
it is all one. The tracks

we pursue are ours;
the zone we would enter

not the mountains, but ourselves.
So for a moment, the mind

may afford to swing out
over the wide abyss.

IV
Then comes the point when body
and mind are one, each indefinable

except in terms of the other.
Head and heart held

in a single nose. The Beast,
the Grey Man, cannot touch us here.

His footprints descending,
identical with our own.

Later, victims of Time and Loss,
we will return and gaze there –

and marvel at such heights
conquered, such blazing air.

Birds of Passage

Why do we keep coming back, year
after year, who do not belong here?
To this rock, where black rabbits abound?
The soil is poor, the lighthouse unmanned.

There is nothing of birth, or possession.
Nor is it entirely the broch, with its sparse
sward and saint's bones. Yet something stronger
than mere habit (so unquestioned

when the time comes) draws us to where
we can see the turnstone swoop, and hear
the mallard massing in the air.

You used to worship, on unbroken knees,
in a village chapel with honeysuckle
ladling the air. I still
have snapshots of you, among the roses.
God's will has strange ironies.

Such energy and gracefulness were yours
it is baffling to see you sit
paralysed to the waist yet
worshipping God who took your gay colours,
with a faith so elemental, fierce.

Watching them wheel you down the aisle, I am humble.
I, who would curse the fate
that has twisted you into what
you are, shudder to hear you say life's ample
for your needs, Christian by such example.

Summer Afternoon

She spends the afternoon in a deckchair,
not moving, a handkerchief over
her head. From the end of the garden
her eyes look gouged. The children stare,
then return to their game. She used to take
them on country walks, or swimming in the lake.
These days are gone, and will not come again.

Dazzling slats of sunlight on the lawn
make her seem so vulnerable; her bombazine
costume fading with each drifting beam.
As the children squall, she imagines
other generations: Is that you, Tom,
or Ian, is it? – forgetting one was blown
to bits at Ypres, the other on the Somme.

Momentarily in pain, she tightens
her lips into something like a grin.
There comes the first rustle of rain.
Carrying her in, you avoid my eye
for fear of interception, as who should say
Shall we, nearing extremity,
be equal objects of distaste and pity?

Yet desperate in the meantime to forbear
for the sake of the love this poor
creature bore us, who was once so dear.

A Sense of Order

Sunday walk

I stop at the foot of Garioch Drive
where my aunt used to live
three floors up.
        I remember the smell
of camomile that hit you in the hall,
the embroidered sampler, the jars
of wax chrysanths, the budgerigars
in their lacquered cage; the ladies who came
to read the Bible in the front room –
surrounded by marzipan, and dragons
on silky screens.
        A rag-and-bone man,
his pony ready for the knacker's yard,
rounds a corner (short of a tail light)
and disappeares up Clouston Street.

Below, the Kelvin runs like stinking lard.

Period piece

Hand in hand, the girls glide
along Great Western Road.
           Outside
the Silver Slipper the boys wait,
trousers flared, jacket-pockets
bulging with carry-outs.

The girls approach. A redhead
pouts, sticks her tongue out,
then passes under the strung lights
to the dance-floor. 'I'll have it
off with that one.' 'Wanna bet?'
'I'd rather lumber her mate...'

They nick their cigarettes.
           Inside,
the miniskirts are on parade,
listening to The Marmalade.

Cranworth Street

I climb the tenement stair
with its scoured tiles, odour
of cat.
     We lived here, before
moving to Ayrshire.
I have not been back, for years.

The brass nameplate, the square
bellpull, mean nothing any more.
What is there to recapture,
to rediscover?
           Too late
in the season, for that.

I cling to the wooden
rail and for no reason
break out in a sweat
as I reach the street.

Street scene

The faces outside the Curlers
explode like fat cigars
in the frosty air.

Even the newsvendor
rocks on his heels, half-seas over.
And I don't blame him.

As the pictures
come out, scores of lovers
head for their parked cars.

Two ladies whisper
goodnight to each other.
Neither feels secure
till on her own stair
she snibs the basement door
and breathes freely, behind iron bars.

Portents

Southpark

The area palls, and its mildewed parades.
    Victorian terraces,
  taken over for the University, lose
their ironwork, their fluted balustrades.

Among the charred bedsteads, the crazy mirrors,
    I keep thinking of those men in dungarees
  putting an axe through Mackintosh's
front door ... Glasgow is in arrears.

The salon

The supporting programme always began
at 5.30. But they didn't open
    till 5.28. So that
by the time you'd got your ticket
    and found your seat
you'd missed the first four minutes.

Once when we could scarcely see the screen
    for fog, we didn't complain –
but sat through the entire programme again.
Phantom cops, after a phantom Keaton.

    In December, the gate
    was locked. The white
frontage peels. The posters are gone
but for a clutch of curls, a crimped grin.

Costume piece

Every morning two women in Edwardian costume
stood for hours opposite the men's Union.
It seemed one or other had been let down
by a medical student: clear water over sharp stones.
When they disappeared, we hoped for a happy
conclusion – only to hear both had been put away.

Botanics

Somewhere, a clock strikes. Schoolboys
    in cherry caps and corduroys
face the death-trap of Great Western Road
    watched by a lollipop-man, then head

for the ice-cream parlour
    and the Gardens – where the keeper,
not wanting trouble, goes inside
    to his prize orchids, his marble nudes.

Behind the hothouse the boys shout
    at an artist in sombrero and tights
too dour even to look up. By the gate
    the winnowing fantails preen and pirouette.

Boudin at the Burrell

Astonishing how his blurry clusters of promenaders
with parasols, washerwomen and shrimpers
wading in the shallows, should be so varied;
especially when rather than venture out to sea
he kept returning to beach and jetty at low tide.

Dreamer and loner, throughout his life he happily
narrowed horizons, enabling us to drink in
those elements he made his own. His secret,
a gift for capturing cloud formations, fine
or bearing rain; their silky turbulence.

Eyeing those bathing-boxes drawn by horses
he was never the voyeur, detesting Trouville's
masquerade of gilded parasites and poseurs. Nor fond
of distances: as lengthy a journey as any when he died
and was transported to be alongside his wife, in Montmartre.

Family Visit

Laying linoleum, my father spends hours
with his tape-measure
littering the floor
as he checks his figures, gets
the angle right; then cuts
carefully, to the music
of a slow logic. In despair
I conjure up a room where
a boy sits and plays with coloured bricks.

My mind tugging at its traces,
I see him in more dapper days
outside the Kibble Palace
with my grandfather, having
his snapshot taken; men firing
that year's leaves.
The Gardens are only a stone's throw
from where I live ... But now
a younger self comes clutching at my sleeve.

Or off to Innellan, singing, we would go,
boarding the steamer at the Broomielaw
in broad summer, these boomps-a-daisy
days, the ship's band playing in a lazy
swell, my father steering well clear
of the bar, mother making neat
packets of waste-paper to carry
to the nearest basket or (more likely)
all the way back to Cranworth Street.

Leaving my father at it
(he'd rather be alone) I take
my mother through the changed Botanics.
The bandstand is gone, and the great
rain-barrels that used to rot
and overflow. Everything is neat
and plastic. And it is I who must walk
slowly for her, past the sludge
and pocked granite of Queen Margaret Bridge.

To My Father

One of my earliest memories (remember
those Capone hats, the polka-dot ties)
is of the late thirties: posing
with yourself and grandfather before
the park railings; me dribbling

ice-cream, you so spick and smiling
the congregation never imagined
how little you made. Three generations,
in the palm of a hand. A year later
grandfather died. War was declared.

In '42 we motored to Kilmarnock
in Alec Martin's Terraplane Hudson.
We found a pond, and six goldfish
blurred under ice. They survived
that winter, but a gull got them in the end.

Each year we picnicked on the lawn;
mother crooking her finger
as she sipped her lime. When
they carried you out on a stretcher
she knew you'd never preach again.

Since you retired, we've seen more
of each other. Yet I spend this forenoon
typing, to bring you closer – when
we might have been together. Part of what
I dread is that clear mind nodding

before its flickering screen. If we come over
tonight, there will be the added irony
of proving my visit isn't out of duty
when, to myself, I doubt the dignity
of a love comprising so much guilt and pity.

Reiteration

What terrifies me is that you should see your death
   reflected in my eyes. Yours are moist, glazed
   over; rimmed with red, as you gaze
at the images on their tiny screen. Beneath

the surface of things, your heart takes
   irregular leaps forward, towards the dark.
   Its rhythms are broken easily; by the van parked
too close for comfort, the fool whose brakes

took him through the Argyle Street
   lights; Lennox's goal in the dying minutes...
   And I think of the pressures youth puts
on age, neither prepared to meet

the other half-way. I remember you beat
   me with a leather belt for using a word
   that can nowadays be overheard
even in your trim Bearsden street.

I swore I'd get my own back
   when I was older, stronger:
   I'd wait till you no longer
had the upper hand, and give you an attack

one way or another. Now I see
   how strengths vary; the grasp
   of one over another depending not on the clasp
of wrist or forearm. You are still stronger than me –

and apart from all else, have more experience
   of death's ways, having watched others go.
   Here in this tiny space, you
stare calmly at what I only dimly sense.

Far from being imprisoned in this room
   which is how I'd seen it, the big guns
   thudding, I realise you've won
more battles than most – and have just one to come.

Reawakening

'Worse than that, the walls smeared
with excrement, adults with the minds
of children, behaving like pigs
at a trough; men circling the yard,
each with a hand on the shoulder
of the man in front. One patient
kept in a padded cell, lest he rape
someone as he did his mother
in '24: the face frozen, body slow
but for the hands' constant fever.'

My father has not broached the subject
of his thesis, *encephalitis lethargica*,
for as long as I can remember. Today
I show him an article in *The Listener*
describing how a new drug has awakened
a group of patients in the States: one woman
paralysed forty years leapt to her feet,
ran round the ward, shattered inmate
and doctor alike – then had to face
being two ages, at the same time.

'Most frightening, the moral decay:
one female student caught the disease
(this confirming its infectious nature)
and soon had the University in a turmoil.
How she ended up, I couldn't say...
Thanks for underlining those sections,
that helps ... The strongest argument I've known
for euthenasia: the wrong side
of the story of the Sleeping Beauty,
no cure known, least of all a kiss.'

Putting the paper aside, he tells
of the research he did; using expressions
he must have thought he'd forgotten;
referring to a thesis that has lain
in a drawer for thirty years:
his mind awakening, at the one time,
to what he did – and what he might have done.

In the Kibble Palace

In the Kibble Palace with its dazzling statues
and glass dome, reading a poet I've just come across,
I learn that under ice the killer whale

seeing anything darker than snow, falls away
then charges, smashing the ice with his forehead,
isolating seal or man on a drifting piece

of the floe. Imagine those tons of blubber
thrusting up; tail curveting
as the hammer head hits. What if the skull

should split, splinters penetrate to the brain?
Nor will dry land protect us from the thudding
in the blood, those forces below. How can we conquer

who cannot conquer ourselves? I shall think of this
when, fishing on frosted glass, I find
my line tightening against the swell;

or hearing you moan and turn in your sleep
I know you are on your own, far out,
dark shapes coursing below. Meanwhile

the horizon closes in, a glass
globe. We will admit it is there
when it is too late; and blunder for the exits

to find them locked. Seeing as though through ice
blurred forms gyrate, we will put our heads
together and try to batter a way out.

Tremors

We took turns at laying
an ear on the rail –
so that we could tell
by the vibrations

when a train was coming.
Then we'd flatten ourselves
to the banks, scorched
vetch and hedge-parsley,

while the iron flanks
rushed past, sending sparks
flying. It is more and more
a question of living

with an ear to the ground:
the tremors, when they come,
are that much greater –
for ourselves and others.

Nor is it any longer
a game, but a matter
of survival: each explosion
part of a procession

there can be no stopping.
Though the end is known,
there is nothing for it
but to keep listening ...

Along the Terrace

Drinks, along the Terrace.
Another marriage, it appears,
is on the slide. Neither party
has anything to hide.

Are we
merely waiting our turn?

In bed
that night, we lie so close
it is impossible to tell
whose is the jumping pulse.

Aquarium

Fishes striped like spinnakers
bob towards us, then blousily
go about. Theirs a dark
world, haunted by bubbles.
Tapping the glass does nothing

to distract them, their steady
intake. Press your face to it,
they merely distort further.
It is as though we were peering
through a two-way mirror;

underwater voyeurs, taking
the tide's pulse as well
as our own. Is this
how it will begin –
when the glaciers melt

and the caves refill?
How it will all end,
as we wait for the kill?
A face is imprinted
on the glass. An attendant

seeming scarcely to breathe
switches out the lights.
Luminous fronds unfurl.
Still no sound. Your ringed
hand comes against mine, clutching.

Bonfire

Relations are strained, again, with next door.
This morning the oldest boy, having broken
one of my wife's favourite shrubs, got
the rough edge of my tongue. (Any
day now, they'll have the wall down.)

So as I light the bonfire, instead of the usual
clutter of children twirling burning paper,
the only acknowledgement is the twitch
of curtains, scowls from behind the pane.
I stack the twigs, pile the dry leaves on.

Soon I am aware of another preoccupation.
Every twenty minutes, a different gentleman
comes from next door; followed shortly after
by a blue-skirted girl, who brings another back.
Slow on the uptake (this being a respectable

neighbourhood) it is only later I realise
she must be on the game. To bring up children
here. I am sickened by a mixture of smoke
and desire. You call that tea is ready.
I run for the door, leave the rake lying.

Very late I go out to check the bonfire.
Two figures move, in the shadow. A radio
blares. A light on the first floor
cuts through scarlet curtains. Where
my heaps of leaves had been, grey embers glow.

After the Party

I drive you home, your seat-belt fastened
to take you in. Your time draws near. Never

have I seen on you such a bloom. Fears skim
the surface. Most remain unspoken. Now

and again though, we talk the next stage through.
The car garaged, I follow you in. Loaded with gifts

we've been given. Who survive by moving
from one house of glass to another.

Before Dark

(for Douglas Dunn)

They are so confident, the young, who strut
    through the avenues that once were ours;
    so sure of themselves, knowing the future is theirs;
so cool and relaxed, as they scale the sweet
    octaves of love; so self-possessed,
    desire not yet on the wane, or become lust.

A bell sounds. The end of lectures for today.
    They fan out across the pastures
    of the city, filling the nearest bars
or returning to bed-sitters, wearily.
    The old smells linger: in Gibson Street,
    curry powder; stale urine, from the Pewter Pot.

In my mind it will always be winter
    in this Victorian sector of the city,
    its terraces squandered by the University,
heaped with swept leaves, a rotting umber;
    Kelvingrove a vast litter-bin; children
    playing, generation upon generation.

I still have black and white snapshots taken
    in front of wrought-iron gates, in the early
    days of the War; my father wearing a kipper tie.
How long I wonder, before our children,
    asked who we were, explain idly if lovingly?
    In old age perhaps the rarest quality –

certainly the one I most envy – is dignity,
    especially in the face of pain. I cannot bear
    the thought of what loved-ones may suffer.
This is partly what drives me to poetry.
    The Missa Solemnis on, we sit and listen:
    From the heart, may it go to the heart again.

Arrivals

I

The plane meets
its reflection on the wet
runway, then crosses
to where I wait
behind plate glass.

I watch
with a mixture
of longing and despair
as you re-enter
the real world.

All we have is each other.
I sometimes wonder
if that is enough;
whether being together
enlarges or diminishes grief.

II

Remember arriving
from Thorame –
the scent
of honey
of lavender clinging.

On the Jonte,
climbing goat-tracks
to drink from a spring
under an arch
of red sandstone.

Or last year,
a second honeymoon
in Amsterdam, having
exchanged gifts: a miniature
war-horse, a silver ring.

III

Tonight your return
from Ulster
renders my fears
unfounded.
Yet neither

of us speaks. Instead
we think of those
living there, others
who have died.
Your brother-in-law

has decided to emigrate:
the one sure escape.
As I draw up
at the lights, you droop
forward, hands on your lap.

IV

The pubs are coming out.
In Dumbarton Road
two drunks, having battered
each other senseless, sit
in their own vomit.

No one interferes.
It is not easy
to accept there may
be a certain mercy
in living here.

The lights turn
to green. I imagine
you lying alone
in a white room, surrounded
by flimsy screens ...

through the murky
water. Under the lattice-work

of white spars, whose
curved glass has

mirrored family upon family,
we too shall soon be,

like my father and grandfather,
ghosts in the empty air.

Seize the Day

Come on Daddy, come now I hear them shout
as I put the finishing touches to this and that

in the safe confines of my study:
Hurry daddy before it's too late, we're ready!

They are so right. Now is the time.
It won't wait, on that you can bet your bottom

dollar. So rouse yourself, get the drift
before you're muffled and left

for useless. *Let's build a snowman, then
a snow-woman to keep him company. When*

*that's finished, and with what's left over,
a giant snow-ball that will last for ever,*

only hurry daddy. As soon as this poem
is finished, I promise, I'll come –

essential first, to pin down what is felt.
Meanwhile the snow begins to melt.

Return Visit

Revisiting the Kibble Palace
after years of absence
is once more to witness
time's destructiveness.

The statues have lost
their piercing whiteness.
The herbage is less dense.
Even the glass dome seems

diminished in circumferance.
To think my grandfather
carried me here; my sons in turn
scouring this pool for goldfish

and silted coins.
Now the lilies have gone.
And look how tawdry
the entrance has become.

When we leave, we cross
the shrunken Gardens,
not glancing behind us.
Later, at a distance,

I concede that what's lost
is within myself: the past
cannot be repossessed.
What future there is, is theirs.

IV

Under the Ice

Like Coleridge, I waltz
on ice. And watch my shadow
on the water below. Knowing that
if the ice were not there
I'd drown. Half willing it.

In my cord jacket
and neat cravat, I keep
returning to the one spot.
How long, to cut
a perfect circle out?

Something in me
rejects the notion.
The arc is never complete.
My figures-of-eight
almost, not quite, meet.

Was Raeburn's skating parson
a man of God, poised
impeccably on the brink;
or his bland stare
no more than a decorous front?

If I could keep my cool
like that. Gazing sraight ahead,
not at my feet. Giving
no sign of knowing
how deep the water, how thin the ice.

Behind that, the other
question: whether the real you
pirouettes in space,
or beckons from under the ice
for me to come through.

In the Gallery

SCOTTISH NATIONAL GALLERY, EDINBURGH

(for Marilyn and James Runcie)

Heading for the National Gallery
to renew acquaintance with the Turner watercolours
I find I am formulating an analogy
between this aesthetic pleasure and the urgency
with which we must face fierce

mortality. For one month only of each year
are these paintings on display,
lest their colours
succumb to the light's rays.
So in marriage, we must seize

every opportunity to act lovingly,
while fire is kept at bay. May
God in his mercy let us share
a little longer the charmed lives we bear.
So I make for these subtle blues and ochres,

illustrations on smooth-grained paper
of weightless lakes and rivers; trees
like plumes, waterfalls suspended in mid-air;
on the bank, tiny transient figures –
only when I get there to discover

today is the first of February.
Accepting this as salutary, I take away
in my mind's eye a graver imagery:
Rembrandt, ageing; and Goya's doctor,
heating his hands under a wintry sky.

Kitchen Maid

Reaching the Rijksmuseum
mid-morning, in rain,
we skirt the main hall
with its tanned
tourists and guides

and, ignoring the rooms
we saw yesterday,
find ourselves heading
past Avercamp's skaters,
Brueghel's masses of flowers

and even the Night-Watch
in its noisy arena
till, up carpeted stairs,
we are in a chamber
made cool by Vermeer.

For what might be hours
we stand facing
a girl in a blue apron
pouring milk
from a brown jug.

Time comes to a stop.
her gesture will stay
perpetually in place.
The jug will never empty,
the bowl never fill.

It is like seeing
a princess
asleep, under ice.
Your hand, brushing mine,
sustains the spell:

as I turn to kiss you,
we are ourselves
suspended in space;
your appraising glance
a passionate embrace.

Visiting Hour

In the pond of our new garden
were five orange stains, under
inches of ice. Weeks since anyone
had been there. Already by far
the most severe winter for years.
You broke the ice with a hammer.
I watched the goldfish appear,
blunt-nosed and delicately clear.

Since then so much has taken place
to distance us from what we were.
That it should have come to this.
Unable to hide the horror
in my eyes, I stand helpless
by your bedside and can do no more
than wish it were simply a matter
of smashing the ice and giving you air.

Afternoon Visit

It is a gusty April afternoon.
    The wrestling is on television,
punctuated by adverts. Her walking, even
    this past week, has slowed down

perceptibly, her leg grown stiffer.
    At one point, getting up
to adjust the set, she overbalances. Before
    either of us can intervene, a cup

and saucer fall to the floor.
    Neither breaks. What does snap,
surprisingly, is her composure.
    Taking her grandchild on her lap

she strokes his head over and over again,
    not noticing the tears
flow. 'Love is the main
    thing. Yet let Nature take its course.

Children are their own. Time must come,
    it cannot be helped.' And strokes
that helpless head. I remember at home
    sitting on her lap, surrounded by books

and ornaments bought over the years,
    most of them to be chipped, at least,
by ourselves as children. 'There's
    no evading it ...' Some fearful beast

within me refuses to listen; would smash
    down the walls, the watercolours
in their frames, the precious trash
    of a lifetime. I am no longer hers,

she is saying – not knowing it
    but speaking simply, without grievance,
from the heart. How can I be fit
    to raise children, I wonder; tense

with foreboding on their behalf and my own,
    who am already a father before
having learned to be a son.
    The child slips to the floor

and plays there. Her eyes mist
    over. I concentrate on the faded green
of an apron. What will become of us, at the last?
    Men fight through blizzards, on the TV screen.

Snowman

Overnight, the thaw came.
All trace of snow had gone
from the gardens. Yet
when I looked out, what
should I see but a snowman
in the middle of the lawn.
I thought of Wallace Stevens'
nothing that is not there
and the nothing that is
and decided to try again
with my glasses on. Sure
enough it was there still,
large as ... well, life. No one
near, or looking even.

Was it a crystallisation
of guilt and desire,
this conjuntion of elements
customarily hidden?
Adjusting focus, I realise
it is some object
wrapped in white polythene.
Before there is a chance
to explore further
a man from next door
hoists it on his shoulder
and carries it in; leaving
only a nagging circle
on the grass where it had been.

Snowfall

Slow thaw

Slabs of snow, stacked against the guttering,
keel on the lip, then slop down
on the tarred tubs littering
the area. Each clearance brings
filthy water, as from a gushet;
a juddering of blocked veins.
We switch off television, sit
watching nothing. Each of us wonders what
to say. Tomorrow we shall have the great
thaw to discuss. Meanwhile there is tonight.

Mid-week

'Like felled logs,' you say. And 'Yes, the alarm
has gone, did you not hear?' A small child charms
us with, 'Open the shutters, so I can see out.'
The mind wallowing from last night's
trough, I go through. The rutted snow
has gone to slush, not frozen. Along the Row
cars start. People pass, looking in.
I switch off the centre-light. Our bin
is on the pavement, on its side,
its lid gone. Is there nothing we can hide?

Japanese bowl

They are bringing the dead off the mountain.
It has been the worst winter for years.
You ask, can we go sledging. In the Gardens
yesterday a father sat his small daughter,
shrieking with laughter, on a new toboggan,
then watched helpless as it careered
downhill into a tree. I still hear
the crack of her skull – and cannot tear
myself from this glazed Japanese
bowl, its surface minutely crazed.

At the Airport

We wave goodbye and watch them go,
loved and familiar figures, through
the security check, and on. In next to no
time, they will descend on Ulster,

a charred land I lay no claim to
other than through them, my parents-in-law.
They used to go by steamer from the Broomielaw;
later, the shorter journey from Stranraer

to Larne. Now the journey is more speedy,
but the gulf between us and the greenery
of Down and Antrim grown immeasureably –
so that what I see when people say

'Get the Army out' are two elderly
heads on a pillow, steeped in blood. To me
if not to most, politics are secondary
to the tug of personal loyalty.

On the periphery of our lives
as they now are of ours,
we will be over the water
when our children are older,

who already have privacies
we cannot share... So much
of life is a biting back of fear.
Their plane is a speck in cerulean skies.

Pentland Poems

Above Glencorse

In the lee of a stunted pine, we pour
coffee from a thermos, adding whisky
to keep out the chill. Perched here
it is hard to escape from history.

Vigorous on the summit of Castlelaw
Scott would tell of Covenanters
joyless on the sward below.
Earlier, startled worshippers

watched a highland soldiery swagger
towards Holyrood; the Young Pretender,
unaware of Derby, impending Culloden,
flicking at flies with a blotched cane.

Breathing deeply, the air keen,
I keep thinking of Stevenson
longing for home. How soon,
in some Samoa of our own,

will we sense the grim-visaged visitor come
and, peering through time,
wonder when next we will, like Cromwell's
men, *eat biskett and cheese on Pentland's hills?*

Westlandman

I lie here, who for Christ's interest did appear
amongst those martyred on Rullion Green,
having trudged from Dumfries through Ayr,
knowing I was unlikely to see my family again;
even then, not anticipating such slaughter
as would befall us, such numbers slain.
All to see the Episcopacy overthrown.

For days, drizzle steamed on a stew of limbs;
those who tried to flee being hewn down
in the mirk, between here and West Linton,
their death-gasps reaching me like an exhalation.
So I lie, deep in Pentland bog, my person
preserved perfectly, my spirit broken.
How many must perish, in God's name?

Lothian burn

Up here, scarcely
birdsong even: only

the labials and gutterals
of this burn as it gurgles

downhill, locality of accent
in vowel and consonant,

each circumlocution
through heather and sandstone

traced by inflection
and sharp interjection

until, in a mossy outcrop,
it comes to a glottal stop.

Moving In

October ends. Against my study wall
the rose-hips shrivel. The central

heating is like leaves shifting
behind the skirting. The boys'

woollens and long stockings
are laid out for the morning.

Since the hour went back
there has been mist, incessant rain.

At dusk the New Town
comes into its own:

a cat at each corner, shady permutations
of wives and lovers gliding through its lanes.

In bed, we cling to one another
and prepare for a long winter.

Offshore

Edging from shingle, the dinghy turns
   a tight half-circle, heading past the island
with its twisted pines, the twin horns
   of rock guarding the bay, out across the sound.

Opposite the lighthouse we ship the oars
   and drift, lopsided. The boys let out handlines,
each hook hidden in plastic and red feathers:
   preferable, they feel, to bait moiling in tins.

Each, thinking he has a bite, finds weed.
   Small hands grow icier, with each haul;
until only hope deferred, and pride,
   sustain them. I wish them mackerel –

but find my thoughts turn, coldly, towards
   the foreign fleets who come
trawling our shores; recalling the words
   of those who say this was a fisherman's kingdom

once, the surface phosphorescent from shoals
   of herring feeding; holds crammed,
decks silver with their scales.
   a bygone age, not likely to return; the unnamed,

as is customary, having destroyed. The boys,
   eyes glistening with weariness and trepidation,
wind in for the last time. Grown wise,
   they know I know there's nothing on the line.

End of Season, Drumelzier

Scarcely discernible, the line tautens
against the current, then sweeps downstream.
The rod-tip shifts, dislodging a thin
gleam of light. I spool in, cast again.

So the season ends. In near darkness
I try to reach the rise.
Something jumps. The circles
are absorbed. Night closes in.

I stumble from the luminescent Tweed
and trudge by torchlight to the farm,
then home: waders discarded, I concentrate
on the winding road; watch hedgerows pass,

sheer banks; branches like weed, overhead.
Sedgeflies smudge the screen. I bear left
towards row upon row of lights that never meet.
In under an hour, I am crossing Princes Street.

So the close of each trout season
brings its own desperation
to make up for lost days; a trek
to the river, a casting more frantic

than judged. In life and love too, take care
to make the most of time – before,
darkness encroaching, it is too late
for anything but the final onslaught.

At the Hairdresser

Behind white astragals, I sit
waiting to have my hair cut.
Soon it will flounce, a greying frazzle, at my feet;
the face in the mirror, sharply lit,
resembling mine, but with more lines
than I'd care to acknowledge, deeply slit
into the features as by theatrical make-up.

All round, women flit – as though part
of some Japanese ritual: brown-smocked,
hair rolled, silent as steam rises
and hot water swirls and plops
in each dazzling sink. Resorting to no tricks
of rejuvenescence, I face facts;
ask simply that it be trimmed, not too short.

On glass-topped tables *Cosmopolitan* and *She*,
sheer gloss, assist the process
of holding time momentarily at bay.
As the scissors snip, I become conscious
of plants in their pots, smooth leaves polished
on the surface but each underside frayed,
marking the tiny red spiders' unyielding progress.

Cherry Tree, at Dusk

The gales have, this past week,
been worse than at the equinox;
leaves spiralling, as though
caught in a thermal; the main bough

of next door's sycamore crazily
overhanging. Through it all, amazingly,
the blossom has clung on:
each bloom, a tiny beacon.

Bedtime Story

'I don't like that one, Hansel
and Gretel, I told them so, little
children enticed by a wicked witch
into her marzipan cottage – such
goings-on – too fearsome
for words, just before bedtime
too: keep them up half the night.'

They recognise her plight,
interpret it differently:
Grandma would be upset, you see
they confide later, from tact:
It's the old woman who gets cooked.

Recovery

I

You know now 'what inhuman pressures
keep a line of verse
on its own course'. The everlasting flowers
shiver in their vase.

And you in a strange place
believing your loved ones
have turned against you.
Behind incandescent mirrors

to be imprisoned...
All I can do is will you
patience and reassurance
and through them, peace of mind.

II

The poet's task, to seek
significant detail
in the face of horror.

It has always been so –
Yeats and Marvell writing
out of disturbance and war.

Like preserving a journal
through plague years.
And consider the chill

chambers, now ruined,
where were produced
those beautiful Books of Hours.

III

Or do you see yourself as Hamlet
in black, on black battlements waiting?
Do you hear the ghost clanking,
the jewelled clock within you, ticking?

Mercifully things are more mundane
on this side of the mirror – no one
plotting to kill you, no cup of poison,
no revenge tragedy, no treacherous queen.

If only the trees outside your window,
bristling with weaponry, could revert
to an uncomplicated green; the tides
off Oban sparkle, as they used to.

IV

It must have been
like winter closing in,
the mind an icy
web; in your case

a sea-loch,
its surface
seeming to freeze
yet retaining

the intellect's finery
and pulsing beneath,
those massive forces,
endurance and love.

At Amersham

(for Kay)

I

Entering the chapel, you survey
for a moment your husband's coffin.
He's gone, after an illness
made less hideous by the devotion
shown in its face. Your coat is green,
his colour. On your wedding-finger
the matching ring from Amsterdam,
where you spent your honeymoon
two years ago. There comes a kind of trembling.
Like a young bride, you walk down
the aisle. The lovelorn bouquets loom.

II

The curtain is closed, the benediction
said. We come out, into the sun.

Your black limousine accelerates down the drive.
Grief is poised in the air, the crest of a wave.

III

In my mind's eye, I see a stretch
of bare beach; on it, the wind
howling, a reed that bends –
and will not snap.

Unicorn Tapestries
(for Meta and Ian Gilmour)

Signaller

They advance, thinking they are unseen;
whereas motionless behind my screen
of walnut, aspen and blue plum
I observe the gloating expressions
of dog-handlers and brocaded Seigneurs,

young noblemen in sumptuous suits
high-stepping it, a jaunty
page-boy pointing gleefully
that the quarry has been sighted.
Not all are participants: witness

the compassion of the old huntsman,
fur hat tied under his chin.
Yet so immediate the brutality,
alongside richness and beauty,
that rather than peer across a chasm

of centuries, you fear to see mirrored
your innermost features: while marvelling
at such floral profusion,
you huddle in your soft-lit ring,
eyes restless, pale faces signalling.

Aftermath

Having visited the Cloisters
with their millefleurs tapestries
we walk through Central Park. Shadows
lengthening, black acrobats

on skateboards, making bird noises,
accelerate from an underpass.
I grasp your hand, try not to run.
Behind sparse shrubbery, huntsmen

hack with pikes; hounds, leashes
slipped, pant with exertion. Could we,
finding a unicorn in the dewy dark,
do more than the mediaeval herbalist

who in his time of turbulence
prescribed, for dogs and others,
distilled primrose water
as a calming influence?

Altarpiece

'For the prior of the Spedale degli Innocente
an altarpiece with these stipulations, namely:

the painting of the panel provided;
powdered gold, to the weight agreed;

ultramarine to the value of four
florins per ounce; the remainder

at the artist's expense. Delivery
within thirty months from today.

Each colour to be mixed by the master
who will carry out the design – in particular

the Holy Family; and make good any failure
or dulling of material, up to ten years.'

The air 'an effete saphire'? Black truly
inferior to white? So say they

who glorify themselves merely; praise
not Art, but preciousness. Against

Bartolo's hierarchy of colour,
I set the harmony of Nature:

best may be plainest.

Ars Longa, Vita Brevis

I

Seated here, Aphrodite, I cannot but
look up your bum. Still I must say
it's a pretty one, so far as it goes.

Has that Sphinx beside you really
not batted an eyelid all those years?
Now that's what I call composure.

II

On the *via sacra*, where Horace encountered
his old bore, I keep my nose in the air

for fear of doing likewise – and pay
the inevitable penalty:

too late to do anything about it,
I find I am ankle-deep in horse-shit.

III

Adalgesa, Zev's housekeeper, rolls the pasta
for dinner. Aged 94, takes the stairs
at a canter. Recently, bemoaning

a lack of sex in her life, was asked
when she'd first noticed. *'Last
night ... then again, this morning!'*

IV

A vessel already full to the brim
I come upon Cupid and Psyche,
and the Dying Gaul, in one room.

Life is there, from the first butterfly
kiss to the torn side, the crushed throat.

Round marble columns, flames flit.

In Monte Mario

I lie staring at the ceiling, unable to sleep.
In the room opposite, surrounded by scalpels
and glass-topped bottles, Ettore restores lovingly
a Bassano landscape clamped to its easel.
Over my bed, in an oval frame, gilt but unadorned,
is a sensuous Madonna ascribed to Leonardo:
the same model as his Virgin
of the Rocks; the tilt of her chin
caught on canvas at the time of the Borgias;
surveying this room, in a Rome torn by explosion;
even in darkness, radiating tenderness.

Her presence makes me more tense than were any
woman of flesh beside me. Each time I stretch
for the light-switch, a single mosquito
settles just out of reach. At last I rise
and tiptoe murderously across the room –
to be drawn back to her portrait. So
exquisite the dilemma: the wiry creature
perches precisely on the nose of the Madonna.

Springtime

In front of me a girl with bare feet,
in a beribboned dress, picks white
flowers in a field somewhere near Pompeii.

Each day I look at her, head straight,
right hand outstretched as she delicately
plucks the stem. Was she there that night

the lava flowed, birds shrivelled in the sky
and lovers turned to ash, where they lay?
If so, what had she done to deserve it?

I wonder, will it ever be
springtime again, the blood flow freely?
Or has man blighted all hope of recovery?

We are on borrowed time, you and I,
and have been from the outset.
All that is left, is to live lovingly.

V

The Luncheon of the Boating Party

I *Alphonse*

'Have you nothing better to do?', calls
my father, not discreetly, as would befit
my station (son of the proprietor, after all)
but in a blacksmith's bellow, spittle flecking
his chin: 'These boats need repairing.' Instead

I lean on the balustrade, observer and observed,
posing for a painting. (When will he understand
it is not seemly to move, once positioned?)
By an artisan too, no mistake about it:
a true painter who finds the term *artist* effete.

How long it could take, God knows. Some *cocotte*
wrote asking to be in it. When she found Angèle
already here, the fur flew. 'Snotty bitch!'
'Just because you sat for Degas!' From our upper terrace
come their voices, across four decades.

And all illusion: the fourteen of us
never together at the one time, far less
spaciously composed. That aside, why make me
so severe, and Caillebotte, seated opposite,
conspicuously fresh-faced? Not that I'm other

than proud to be there: look how many (a Baron
included) it took to counterbalance me.
Most astounding, the light: no criss-cross of shade
under the striped awning, but a steady suffusion.
The way he depicts it forces me to re-remember.

'That must be the boatman,' I suddenly overhear,
'waiting till luncheon's over, to ply his trade.'
'Or Charon, envisaging the placing of coins,
in due time.' Not dreaming I'd catch the reference,
or realising how, uppermost in my mind

and complementing those succulent flesh-tones,
was Renoir's skin, even then tightening on his bones
like canvas stretched over the frame of a painting;
as in one of those pleasure-boats, long-since gone,
he would sit, to be rowed across the dappled Seine.

II *The Baron*

Why should he complain? What about me?
The back of my head's about all you see,
precious little else. Whereas if he'd chosen,
Renoir my dear old pal, to survey the scene
from the other end of the terrace, I'd have been

smack in the centre. With his back to the Seine.
Then he could have called his painting
Baron Barbier, cavalry officer and bohemian,
lunching with friends at the Restaurant Fournaise:
if I'd been presented full phiz, that is,

not in this retiring fashion. Between you and me
I was in fact facing him, when he began. Only
to let myself be distracted by that 'unknown
model' (the catalogue calls her) leaning over
the balustrade, ogling in my direction.

Actually her name was Maxine. I could fill you in
more fully, if you want, but don't see why
I should do her any favours when she did me none.
There she is, a nonentity preserved for posterity,
whereas I am virtually relegated to 'Anon'.

And in one of the finest paintings ever painted,
it would seem. Not that anyone dreamed that
at the time. Indeed when the moment came
to cough up, Monsieur Balensi (it seems) renaged
on the deal. I thought she was egging me on

(Maxine, that is) but it turned out all she was after
was what she could glean about my friend Maupassant.
As for that haughty buffoon, the proprietor's son
(back to him again) let me tell you something.
He was damn near not even in the picture. Renoir

painted him out, then in again, after asking him
to take off his jacket and wear a white singlet.
Do you know why? In order to highlight
the flowers on a straw hat. As though we existed
purely for his still life. What do you make of that!

III *Unknown man*

'Out there,' they said, 'on the terrace –
you're wanted.' Hearing the din
I assumed it was those oarsmen again,
kicking up a shindig. Not a bit of it –
there were some of the regulars

and a man with a pointy beard,
painting them. 'That's perfect,' he said,
'don't worry about your arms, so long
as you face in this direction.' I was only
a bit player, I realise. All the same

it was fun, to be one of them.
I well remember the conversation –
even the chaps whispering smutty jokes
to the girl with black gloves.
At one stage she covered her ears

from embarrassment. I could tell
they were both trying to get off
with her. But Renoir made it look
as though she was straightening her hat.
Such a pure spirit, to go through life

confronted by all those nudes –
complete waste, ask me. Mind you
he did, even then, have a crush
on the girl with flowers in her hat
and married her later, I gather.

Anyway, we were simply a job-lot
transformed by his painting. One laugh:
as fast as the wine went down,
his brush replenished it – Art
can't get more practical, than that.

As for the fellow in the top-hat,
I couldn't make out a word
he said. Might have been
from another planet. Mind you,
it was a magical afternoon.

IV *Madame Renoir*

Curiously enough, seeing that painting again
awakens in me not visuals so much as fragrances:
the bouquet of red wine, those grapes and peaches
in the dish under my nose; Alphonse's breath
from over my shoulder, as he munches garlic;

and the mustiness of that stupid little dog
Renoir made me hold: I'm sure it gave me fleas.
Maggiolo poured wine down its throat
for a joke – not expecting it to get its own back
which it did, biting his finger to the bone.

It must have been all in his head, from the start.
Not that you'd have known. Empty glasses and litter
everywhere; the clash of cutlery, bottles quivering...
Oh yes – the women's perfume, that comes back;
Angèle's lily-of-the-valley, something of the sort;

Ellen's sultry and spicy, like bruised fruit.
I wore rose-water, which I knew Renoir fancied.
'It makes a unity of the senses,' he said,
'with the flowers adorning your hat;
symbol of maidenhood.' I was naive enough

to believe him, I think. How ironic,
to be preserved on canvas, in full bloom,
while the body fails – most of all that
of our creator; hands deformed, the brush
strapped to his wrist with bandages

that he might paint. A whole world has gone,
never to return. Including those luxurious
days at Chatou. He always worked from the heart;
gave more than he took. Despite what they say
about him not paying his models: why should he,

when he was making them eternal?
As for me, that time is best recaptured
when I sit beside him in his wicker chair
and sense in his eyes – despite the pain –
a loving tenacity; light glancing on water.

V *Renoir*

Coarse blotches, suggestive of putrescent flesh,
was how they described my *'impressions'*
in those early days. No wonder every so often
Monet and I to escape would stuff ourselves
with larded turkey, washed down with Chambertin.

They protested, 'How can we go by other
than what is seen?' Oblivious
(so much for their breadth of vision)
that the eye ultimately sees
not through itself, but by some other thing.

(What shame anyway, in feasting heart *and* eye?)
Further irony, in my never contriving to be
the revolutionary they would have preferred.
My dream of harmony, not anarchy, all those years
I tried simply to mirror nature, to give joy.

Then there were those who in my intoxication
with female flesh saw an unbridled passion
mirroring some lust of their own – whereas
detecting in breasts and buttocks a purity as well
as beauty, I caressed with brush-strokes alone.

Their trouble, that they allow only one shade
of black, to indulge their curdled spirits.
Ignoring the shadowy blues and greens
which delight the senses, they deride red's redness;
any notion of colour sounding like a bell.

In years to come, carping critics forgotten,
my portraits will sing of Angèle and Ellen,
Gabrielle and Suzanne. If nothing else,
I will have preserved them on canvas: my strength,
and weakness. Meantime, my beloved already gone,

I find it difficult to recollect those days.
Lying twisted under this wire contraption,
I watch the bones work their way through my skin.
Soon, I shall be beyond pain. All labour done,
there will be no paints to mix, no brushes to clean.

[Les Collettes, 1991]

114

At Les Collettes

(for Serge Baudot)

Scarcely any distance from the peopled *plages*
extending their pebbled curve to Menton
and beyond, under the broiling Mediterranean sun,
leave the boulevard and climb by the Passage Renoir
to *Les Collettes*, built for my final years.

In the hour before the house opens for the afternoon.
stroll round the gardens, under those knotted olives,
themselves a vast age before we came to occupy the place.
Shade your eyes, as I had to, and look across
the chasm of light between here and the château

of Cagnes. Imagine me being wheeled down
these paths in my wooden chair, or sitting hunched
over that day's canvas, in my open-air studio.
Then enter the house, and experience its coolness.
Go up (as I could not, latterly, unaided)

to the *atelier* on the first floor, and look down
as I constantly did, on the powdery green
of the olive trees. Consider them if you care,
with their gnarled contortions, a metaphor
for my deformed hands' durability, through pain.

*

Fortunately I had too much to keep me busy
to worry about Cézanne and Matisse and the others
'changing the face of Art'. As I gather
turned out the case. I always kept to a sole design;
whereas they saw from several vantage points, at once.

Not only that, but they'd detect prisms
and angles, where I saw only smoothness.
I sometimes wondered what chaos it caused,
especially when that dark-eyed young fellow Picasso
(born the year I did my *Déjeuner des Canotiers*)

came bounding like a goat, on the scene,
promising to go further than even their extremes;
painting what he *thinks*, not what he *sees*.
One clear reason why, rather than contemplate
the future, I was happy to remain in the present.

For all that, I admit (in trust) to a desperation
that once what is new has been superceded
by the 'new' new, my early work, derided
at the time, may be seen in true perspective;
it be conceded I opened shutters, let light in.

*

Sleep comes over me. I have been too much in the sun.
And begin to be overtaken by a kind of delirium.
Purveyor of order, resident in this rectilinear mansion,
so meticulously terraced, I see myself at times
as comprising a geometry of my own: a sundial

round whom revolve fragrances, subtleties
of brightness and shade, which I transmute
to canvas, in a process most easily
attributed to sheer *joie de vivre* –
if only to put the culture hounds off the scent.

They could not comprehend for instance, how Aline
dictated her own style. Not least, through my delight
in her rotundity: midway between fantasy
and reality. More splendidly too, than with any
other model, her skin responded to the light.

Even that now a secondary consideration,
I miss her so much. Above all, the softness
of her fingers, as she wound the bandages on.
This, among my memories, the one thing
that dulls the pain. I wish she were with me again.

Renoir in Orkney

Monet might have made himself at home
among these flat, green islands
like giant water-lilies. Cézanne even,
with cliff-faces all cones and cylinders.

Not that my vision is impaired –
more a narrowing of the spectrum
to a harmony of glistening silk
as if too much light were being let in,

but without the embracing warmth
to which I am accustomed: seascape
and skyscape, a constant radiance.
It would need the skin of the place

to burst a blood vessel, or myself
to stab at it with a palette knife:
then there'd be something I could express.
Only this morning the world disappeared;

the boat I was in surrounded
by quicksilver, the bordering land
erased in mist. Like a composer
frantic for some variation

beyond a single high-pitched note
sustained in his brain,
I crave a cacophony of colour,
before my mind disintegrates.

At least with the fisherman
I am at home. Their tanned features
merit the mixing of pigments:
my yellows and reds are in business again.

As for the womenfolk, baiting the line
has made their fingers like my own
and worse: knife-gashes to the bone...
Nudes are out. For one thing, their

Kirk concedes no such tradition.
For another, contemplate the climate.
But something in me burns. I must
start again. I have found a girl

with skin like mother-of-pearl;
am working on still lives of lobsters;
and will distribute at the solstice
canvases of wild flowers, like mottled flame.

Burial Mound

Entering Maeshowe we have to bend double
for the narrow passage which brings us
to the main chamber, in whose recesses
lodged the bones and ashes
of the dead. Torch flitting from ceiling to wall

my guide recites the history of the place,
revealing chiselled runes
on slate slabs, before the beam moves on.
Hesitantly I ask, please could she
cast light again on the inscriptions:

Ingibiorg is the fairest of women;
Hermuntnr of the hard axe carved these –
I ought not to have spoken.
She stops abruptly and with a frozen
clearing of the throat, recommences

from the beginning, without expression
but faster, permitting no further
interruption. Later she lets me examine
briefly the rows of stick-figures,
leads me to daylight again.

Tonight we lie, you and I, darkness a dome
overhead. At least we are together,
our love a live thing, this room
not yet ransacked by whatever invader
will carve here, as on cold stone, his name.

Monflanquin

We follow the track to Monflanquin,
on either side the sheen of rippling grain,
past the graveyard with its flaked stone

and flowers preserved under bell-jars.
As we stand here a coach drawn by white horses
glides past. Is that the music of the spheres

and is it too part of a fantasy,
like the quivering pantiles, the sky
too blue to be real? Try though we may,

it is difficult in such an atmosphere
to realise we are no longer
the definitive selves we once were.

Such timelessness cannot last.
Before they go to waste
or become things of the past

on our return to more mundane
surroundings, the diurnal routine,
within us let us jealously retain

those moments by that honey-coloured château
where we stood arm in arm, as from an upper window
came soaring the overture to *The Marriage of Figaro*.

Fort Napoleon

We sit entranced in the night air
watching a troupe of eight
actresses alternate as Alice,

the dew so heavy they slither
on the stage, till one goes barefoot
and the others follow suit. Finally

they vanish, leaving only the moon's
refractions – and a filigree
of drenched prints, where they had been.

Lot-et-Garonne

This the domain of fable, of ant and grasshopper,
invisible cicada and cackling jay. Facing
due east, the sunflowers shrivel. Over meadows
of maize, loop liquescent catherine-wheels.
Meanwhile in the arena between my feet
two crimson beetles, linked tail to tail,
tug one another across baked soil.

Surfeit of fruit; a season's abundance:
nectarine and peach in profusion; bruised
melon, going cheap. So we stroll, and buy.
Bergerac for today's trout, *vin de table*
for tomorrow's *ragout*. Cheese too, *du pays*.
But keep being drawn to those fruit vendors,
bare arms steeped in wasp-teeming wares.

An hour's cycle-run through shaded groves,
the Château de Biron emerges dominant
on the skyline, visible for miles around.
Severe but for its chapels. Its most
renowned Seigneur beheaded by Henri IV:
now centuries later, bleached bone
in blood-drenched soil. The sky porcelain.

Below, Lacapelle-Biron bakes. Our bicycles
against a wall, we bring out water-bottles
to slake our thirst. Under cypresses, solitary
Protestants lie. The air resonates, like a bell.
A woman waters begonias; while across the square,
a sandstone dog grins – his haunches
so yellow, he could be carved from butter.

A dragonfly settles on my shoulder, a flicker
of azure. Even under lime and acacia,
the glare becomes scarcely tolerable. Last
night's thunder did not long clear the air.
So much, so soon to be distanced from.
Already in the orchard has begun
the steady thud-thud of ripe fruit falling.

Picture Framer

He takes a sliver of beaten gold,
specially prepared; extends it
on a knife-blade, steady handed
and scarcely daring to breathe,
over the frame he is working on;

then with a simultaneous
exhalation and practised
flisk of the wrist, sends
it floating – to land face up
on precisely the right spot:

the gesture repeated,
with what seems
sublime indifference,
till the task is complete;
the frame lustrous, immaculate.

So is love, even after
a lifetime's experience,
at the mercy of flights
as hazardous as those
of gold leaf, through draughts of air.

Aria

Three feet down, in the clarity of Loch Eddy,
a rainbow trout sluggishly avoids the fly
on offer. Our rowing-boat drifts on, with scarcely

a ripple. Suddenly the surface quivers:
the fish leaps into the air, then splashes
back on its belly. As though you, lying there

in drugged sleep, were totally to ignore
my kisses, a moment later to reappear
singing an aria from *Cosi fan Tutte*.

Boat Trip

The motor-boat cuts a swathe across the Sound
as on taut silk, to deposit us on the Island.
We head for a vantage point, tiptoing between
gulls' nests, each with its speckled contents,
ignored by the parent birds – whereas terns or skuas
would instantly have had the scalps off us.

We munch cress sandwiches, the melons we brought.
Pairs of eider go burbling past. Seals
flip-flop from the rock, keeping cool.
Morar emerges from haze. On our return journey
we pass through tangles of *lasagna verdi*
and whorls of liquorice, still unharvested.

Later in an oblong of heat trapped
by the cottage wall, you could close your eyes
and be in Provence almost: the bouquet
of bramble wine, aroma of wild thyme,
scarcely comprehensible in conjunction
with the peat stacks, those peaks on the skyline.

Make the most of it. Soon it will become
another memory, a fiction of its own.
That night the storm breaks; and I hear
Flaubert howl, knowing his Emma, no more
than artifice, an array of imagined syllables,
would long after his death remain alive and real.

The Boathouse

The boathouse is the worse for wear: cracked
pantiles let in rain; a shutter is unhinged, the pocked
weather-vane broken by some local sharp-shooter.
The landing-stage too has seen better days,
its boards rotting. Yet we visit whenever we can
this fading Estate, skirting the big house
and the love temple, with its beeches and planned
rhododendrons. One man has taken the place of eight
gamekeepers. Nor do minor royalty come as they did,
to bag the deer or hold their swinging parties.

Envisage the locals, deferential; the young
gentry, on holiday from boarding school
in the south, disporting themselves nightly.
See the ice-buckets bead, the champagne flow.
The wendy-house on the island, overgrown now,
must have seen many a Chekhovian scene,
or Bacchanalian, girls in flimsy dresses,
hair gossamer in the breeze; sheep's carcasses,
breeding maggots on which the brown trout fed,
straddled on wires across the water's surface.

Strange that our presence should overlay theirs
as we manoeuvre our clinker-built boat in pursuit
of stocked rainbows where, in early summer,
the mountain-ash extend their candelabra.
What will the future bring? Can one owner
with propriety retain such inherited *grandeur*?
Yet how transfer so inaccessible a property,
as some would decree, to the downtrodden?
No ready solution. Our own, who knows,
may come to be counted among 'those balmy days'.

Two Harrier jets wheel overhead; a reminder
of other priorities. Their roar lingers
long after they disappear. Time to row in.
The boathouse shimmers, in the aftermath of rain.
A mink, predator of a different order,
swims to the bank, a fish in its jaws.
In the subsequent near-silence,
intensified by our bow-ripple, I realise
we have not seen or heard the peregrine
this season: like ourselves, an endangered species.

Amber

In an antique shop in the Lawnmarket,
    among lacquered trinketry and ivory
figurines, are five amber apples
    the size of a half-fist: each a source
of wonder, below its translucent surface.

The dealer who unearthed them must care
    as little for their future
as their past – letting them gather dust
    in this window, whose syrupy light
spills across grey cobbles. Imagine them

round the neck of a billowing contralto
    or goitred senator's wife. If pearls drip,
these are a thunder-plump. Too gross
    for any ordinary voluptuary, they'd have graced
Clytemnestra there by the pillar, the axe bare;

or been baubles fit for a temple cat:
    having already survived from primordial
gloom, sucked down and glacially compressed,
    then washed to the shore. Today's pine forests
await their turn, oozing globs of resin.

Passion Fruit

'This is the genuine site of the Garden of Eden.'
Who are we to doubt it? The guide drones on.
'Eve's apple, at least, proffers no problem:
contemplate if you will, the passion-flower fruit.'

Persuasive enough, in the fragrant gloom.
A rustling at the glade's cool rim
conveys the serpent's progress. 'As your party
leaves, you will receive gifts of passion fruit.'

Despite the light's apparent purity,
not one of my transparencies came out.
And at Los Angeles, on my flight
home, they confiscated the passion fruit.

Renewal Notice

Our renewal notice offers cover
against falling trees, hitherto
act of God. A few nights ago

next door's sycamore narrowly
missed. What of the roar at seances,
similar to crumbling upper storeys?

We hear on the News of doors
burst open, three elders gunned
down, women and children maimed;

calls for retaliation we cannot
condone – yet do not wholly
condemn. Next day not even Corelli

unravelling on Radio Three
can erase from the mind
those worshippers crouched behind

flimsy pews in a pentecostal hall.
The blue sky appallingly banal,
shears snipping, you trim the ivy on the wall.

W.S. Graham

I imagine you
  in the woods near Madron,
waiting for the barn-owls to flutter
  and whoo, then swoop down

to take you on yet
  another of these mysterious journeys
you will tell us about
  later, your phrases

so perfectly turned and weightless
  they'd defy gravity
but for the ice
  that pins them in place. Sydney

I wish you well, this
  night and any other
as in your thermal you rise
  through thin air – or

far out from the coast
  in a different manner
find yourself driving
  the last tram from There to Here.

Bird of Passage

(for Tom Leonard)

ALEXANDER WILSON: *b.* Paisley, Scotland 1766;
d. Southwark, Philadelphia 1813

The starlings that roosted in Paisley Abbey's
squat hulk, accumulating layers of lime,
have long since gone, without recognising
the *rara avis* to whom late last century
a statue was raised: Alexander Wilson,
who flew through life like a highly coloured bird.

For chastising such silky muck-worms
as his Hollander who resisted Reform,
and scoun'rel Shark, trig in his powdered
wig, measures fixed to cheat his weavers,
Wilson was hounded by a less than enamoured
constabulary. Plucking his tail feathers,

they locked him in the tolbooth; his verses,
a friend to Liberty, suppressed and burnt.
After Thomas Muir's transportation,
the judiciary preparing its grapeshot,
he felt it wise to jump bail, sailing by way
of Portpatrick and Belfast for Philadelphia.

Jack-of-all-trades but unable to endure
life's collisions, he scraped a living; till
he fell for the warbler's song, the allure
of orchard orioles, their nests suspended
from twigs on fibre hooked and wound
with an ingenuity he, a weaver, had to admire.

Warming to the task of a lifetime
he persuaded a publisher to take on
his magnum opus, *Birds of America*;
seeking subscribers by horse and canoe,
from the St Lawrence to the Mississippi;
meeting Jefferson and Thomas Paine.

A woodpecker, locked in his Wilmington
hotel-room, made a start on a mahogany table;
while a kite, sinking a talon to the bone
and released by severing a sinew of its heel,
confirmed *its* existence. A phantom
flycatcher, his sole aberration, purloined

by Audubon. Father of American Ornithology,
did he ponder the perplexed cartography
of Renfrewshire; engravings untinted,
new species unnoted, had he not departed?
Later, as he lay dying from dysentry
brought on by swimming in pursuit

of a wounded plover, did his thoughts migrate
to the Abbey grounds where he stands
opposite Robert Tannahill, friend
and fellow-poet, who unable to find a publisher
stepped into the Candren Burn, top-coat
folded on the bank, silver fob-watch beside it?

Bird Songs

Starling

Leave me be, to chirp those
notes natural to me. Why should I
aspire to the nightingale's RP,
the career cadences
of thrush and blackie?

I'm merely the back-court piper
of gable walls, fag-end
of a raucous tradtion;
chatterer on roof-trees,
see it how you please.

Nor am I wholly aloof: the others
may not be my cup of tea,
but I'll sit on a fence-wire
all day, listening happily
as their songs pass me by.

Bittern

Think of the years I threw away, down there,
intent on selling my wares, when all they cared for

was the phony falsetto of canaries in cages
or at a pinch, the Home Counties dawn chorus –

twitterers in hedgerows. Such expenditure
of energy: I'd have changed register

even, to fit in. But those days are gone.
Life began again, when I joined the brass section.

Resident

Finding a convenient five-barred gate
  I hitch a trouser-leg up and adopt
  a proprietorial pose: trouble is,
  I can't keep my face straight.

For one thing I haven't the right garb,
  and however levelly I gaze out
  am not even an absentee landlord,
  more a temporary tenant, this visit.

That apart I still carry the flab
  I'm here to get rid of: I'll acclimatise
  as soon as my boots are broken in,
  and the war with the horse-flies is won.

Conspicuous meantime, in a landscape
  complete without me, I'll make a start
  by cutting the grass, in the hope
  of damping that wren's derisive flute.

Skye Poems
(for John and Bar Purser)

On arrival

Here for a break, to shake the mind free
from its dullness, I gaze out on a sea
alternately dazzling with troughs of light
and lost in mist. As I sit and write
you work away, literally overhead,

scraping your cottage's corrugations
with an old hoe, prior to applying tar.
Your implement grates and grates, so close
I feel I'm a turtle or some such creature
having its shell cleaned, barnacles forcibly

removed, with the detritus of the past.
Below, the Bay glistens fitfully.
Bright thoughts force an entry. Soon
the new man that I am must venture
outside, skull scoured, legs however unsteady.

Dawn, Drinan

I lie dozing in the early hours,
aware of some element missing.
Then it comes: a burst of hail
blattering on the corrugated iron
of the roof, like a blizzard
of rock-chips, before expending
itself on the shore at Kilmarie.

Dizzied, I recall the scramble
from Coir an Lochain to the ridge;
our straddling Sgurr Dubh na Da Bheinn,
a sheer drop beyond. The shower passes
as unexpectedly as it came.
Opening my eyes I see the room re-form,
the curtain opposite slowly redden.

Reminder

What remains of today's skyline
is enhanced or marred, according
to viewpoint, by this home-made chair.
Roofed over in Spartan fashion,
its circular peep-holes enable land
on one side, sea on the other,
to recur. Position it, climb in,
you have a sun-trap to boast of;
protection for inclement weather;
a bird-hide, for the eager visitor;
sentry-box even, its driftwood
thicker than any arrow-head. The one
concession to modernity – castors,
for mobility. Upended and fronted
it could prove an economic coffin,
were one to sit upright, not lie down.
Before leaving, I am to put it
in the peat-shed, for its proper safety.

Sabbath

Overnight the wind shifts
from south-west to north-east:
we are into a new season.
The Tourist Board seals
sunning themselves in Loch Slapin
have taken the money and run.

Those mountains that looked as if
you could lean out and touch them
have come clean: they were
contours in the imagination.
The blueness of the other side
might have been invented.

And it's the sabbath. Well, serve
it right – all week the Blackface
have been looking down their noses
like Wee Frees, at a spritely pigeon
with a birch-twig in its beak
masquerading as a dove of peace.

The islanders to the newly-weds

This gift is for you, its graded shades
of grey drawn one from each breed
of sheep on our Island – the wool undyed.

It will require to be teased and spun,
thereafter woven to whichever design
meets your fancy. Before then

there are the fitting means
of preparing the tweed. True romance
decrees the ritual of the dance:

place in a tub, cover with water;
then tread with vigour, the pair
of you, for not less than eight hours.

During the process, such activity
permitted as conforms with propriety.
We wish you happiness. And energy.

Bog myrtle

Evenly spread on bunk beds
in the room above, bog-myrtle lay
drying – till it was taken south

for beer-making. What lingers
is its scent – so that I imagine
some young couple trysting here

(not Diarmid and Grainne, but a less
fated pair), a blessing on them:
legacy of its fragrance, in the air.

Meanwhile I'll leave this poem between
the sheets. Will it curl curiously,
or just fade away? We'll see.

VI

Arrival, Rivonia

My room overlooks an oval pool, lit from below.
Between one and the other, trelliswork of vine.
Such the drought, the perimeter a dust-track.
Lemon and pomegranate trees. On the verandah
azure-necked peacocks strut and squawk.

On my first day I am taken to Melrose House,
site of the signing of the Treaty of 1902.
These Kitchener's quarters. I picture his rigid frame
and incongruous round him, a ring of pretty
officers with butterfly-nets cavorting on the lawn.

The jacarandas have no bloom, being out of season.
On the return journey, the car picking up speed,
we pass brightly clad Blacks in the backs of vans
or at bus-stops, lying back in what shade there is.
Otherwise they only occasionally impinge – as when

heading for the theatre in Johannesburg
we swerve to avoid a black youth, another
prancing round him with a knife.
In the wing-mirror, I see them rock together
as though caught in an irresistible slipstream.

Meanwhile the parasols on the verandah
fade in the sun to a uniform pastel.
Distant barking of dogs; a reminder that the world
still spins. Was this once jungle? I turn,
half fearing to find some creature savaged in the pool.

Sights and Sounds

From my Cape Town hotel, an incessant
barking of dogs; in the Malay Quarter
the muezzin's interminable wail.
I twitch the curtain: a cockroach scuttles.
The preposterous sun splits Signal Hill.

Soon on the car radio, the mellifluous tones
of the English Service tell of the release
on Robben Island of an undisclosed number
of penguins; heavy news, in Afrikaans;
and on Springbok, 'the Rise and Shine Show,

setting you on your way, this Wednesday'.
Past the Hospital Bend intersection
where the accident rate, many years ago,
dropped temporarily with the installation
of a sign, 'Dr. Barnard is waiting for you'.

Domains fragrant with thyme and rosemary;
then Groot Constantia, balm to the eye,
its facades exquisite as sugar-ice
against an azure sky. All porcelain
and honeyed furniture. Upstairs, a clutter

of Edwardiana: old 78s, gramophones
with the original horns. Tempting
to put them on, throw open the windows
and let loose a cacophony ranging from
'Now is the hour' to 'Excerpts from *Lohengrin*'.

Soweto Photographs

(for Bernard Spong and Rykie Woite)

I

Entering Soweto, we pull up to photograph
the contrasting sides of the street: huts
of corroded metal, opposite shacks even older,
squatting in their own detritus. Half
naked children play among rubber tyres.
A dog grapples with a hoop of wire.

A car draws in: a plainclothes patrolman
in shirt and slacks, gun-butt showing.
He asks the driver's occupation.
'Minister of religion ... my friend
from abroad is keen to see round.'
He gestures dismissively. We drive on.

II

Outside the United Congregational
pre-school nursery, twenty children
by means of a plastic mickey-mouse
are taught the words for different colours
in a language not their own. When they get over
the novelty of my presence, I take my pictures

then saunter self-consciously to the street.
There screeches up a van, from which dangle
men in balaclavas: they leap off, empty
dust-bins, are on again and away.
A coalman reins up, wets his eyebrows
and poses as if to say, *Take me, Take me...*

III

'Down there, all that remains
of Sophiatown ... remember Huddleston,
the bulldozing?' Smoke obscures the sun.
Next, Tutu's house: the brave one.
And on, and on. Soon we approach
Orlando Stadium for which

in '76, the children were heading.
My guide saw the bodies lying,
bullets in their back. For the anniversary
next month, police will congregate
on this waste ground, truncheons
and canisters of tear-gas at the ready.

IV

The faces of the elderly,
runnelled as by long drought;
children caught between one moment
and what the next may bring –
hard to believe these photos
are of the Soweto I saw:

squalid browns, even the brick latrines
picturesque in a way that lessens
their power to horrify, defusing
the rage that should augment
pity. What, I ask my companion,
does one do? *'What little one can.'*

V

Last, a child in a blue tee-shirt,
the lower part of his body bare.
In this light the side of his head
seems cropped. He stares
gravely as I peer
at him, get him in focus ...

Now he is on my study wall,
where I tilt at meaningless
windmills, far from his hell.
Huge-eyed, he touches the heart.
Meanwhile, in another murderous
dawn, the world prises itself apart.

[1984]

House Guest

I let myself in
and in the gathered gloom
pour a glass of wine
and make for the sitting-room

where I become aware
of a clicking
too regular
for twigs against the pane.

Telling myself, too metallic
for snake,
I sidle to the door,
switch the light on.

A caged hamster,
pure white with ruby eyes,
circles ceaselessly
in his treadmill of wire.

Stopover in Botswana

Early morning, in Gabarone. Familiar
sounds assume a resonance of their own.
Distant dogs howl. Cocks crow,
presaging a dawn it is hard,
in such darkness, to believe will come.

Leaving by way of Lobatsi,
and east. At the border a man
cracks a hide whip at an imaginary
victim; and the Toyota in front of me,
hitting a mirage-patch, rides on air.

Attractive Swartruggens slips by.
Beyond Rustenberg I book in
to an unsavoury hotel where
I become another brand of alien:
an *Engelsman* at the heart of Afrikanerdom.

So Botswana recedes in the memory,
comprising part of what supplants it –
itself superceded in turn
by the evolving pattern of the whole.
In my morgue-like hotel bedroom

I shrink at the pounding roar
from a shunting-yard; not the din
but the brute force it manifests;
and an awareness, the cocks still crowing,
of the imminence of that savage dawn.

Outsider

(for Jeremy Cronin)

Reading the poems you gave me, I marvel
at a resolution beyond my comprehension,
the lyrical intensity
governing what you have to say.

And face pressed helplessly
against my hotel-room window
am unable to eradicate
from my mind the plate glass

through which for one quarter
of an hour, on the day
your wife died, you saw her mother
sobbing, and could not comfort her.

To what
can one cling, when monstrosity
exists beyond reason?

Pigeons beat
their wings and walk heel-toe
on the roof below.

The Lutheran Church opposite
is tiered like a wedding-cake,
against a dark sky.

Whose knife is at whose throat?

On the Water

(for Gus and Nicky Ferguson)

An opportunity to observe close-up
those exotics I've been peering at
through binoculars, this past week:
the paradise fly-catcher, long tail
unmistakable; loerie with beaded eye;
most delicate, the lilac-breasted roller.
While I puzzle how to translate them
into print, a precocious bee-eater
settles on my pencil, as though
urging a place be found for him, too.

*

I stalk a crimson-breasted shrike,
willing him to come my way. Suddenly
in front of me he hops closer,
all neck-quirk, a blur in the lens:
I zoom in – missing him altogether.
A perfect opportunity muffed
through poor technique,
I go trawling the bird-book
for the finer points. But first
unfold my checklist, make another tick.

*

Beyond the inner circle of ibis and egret:
a decrepit stork who has lost all dignity.
Little more than a scrag of tatters
on a pole, he displays life's scars,
his once sleek jacket now a filthy misfit.
Pocked by puncture-marks, he is patently
an embarrassment. What they are saying to him,
conscience tells me, is 'Get out of it,
and take your cardboard box with you,
before you further lower the tone of the place.'

*

An irascible hornbill casts
a jaundiced eye, can't quite
credit it, so casts another.
Extends head and neck upwards
to emit vertical streamers
of sound. A second responds,
distance an irrelevance: like
Italian tenors, supposedly
addressing one another, but in reality
each playing to the back of the house.

*

Nesting marabou observe with an hauteur
ill becoming their role as scavengers,
seemingly unable to take in that they
and those others irradiating the air
are on the periphery of the action.
The jacana even, stilting dextrously
across the water-lilies, no more
than the *corps-de-ballet* for a purple
gallinule performing, faster than the eye
can take in, *entrechat* upon *entrechat*.

Interior

The tent resisting the night's chill,
I lie dreaming of giraffe and zebra,
kudu and princely sable. Above all
last night's elephant at the water-hole,
bearing the spirits of his ancestors.

Now the canvas panels glow: blue,
red and white – a cubed drapeau;
then to the howl of whirled
acacia, transporting the spirit,
as in a box-kite, high over Africa.

Pilanesberg

The thornveld is shielded from outside
by a raised lava rim; our camp, within
the stone circle of an Iron Age site.
Inside that, a ring of expended ash:
a dead trampoline – the world's navel.

Morning and night, all snake-fang.
But now an approaching whirlwind
sucks spirals of dust into the air.
No escape, should its crazy zigzag
turn our tamed beast to cavortings of fire.

Leopard

We stop with a jolt. Scarcely thirty feet away,
a dapple of light becomes a leopard in a fig tree;
hind-legs dangling, rosettes orange and russet.

So insouciant his descent. All muscular nonchalance,
he flows straight for us. Stops, and stares.
We absorb the amber of those wondrous eyes. Last

night's kill guzzled, he scrapes bloodstained grass.
Is gone. Such masterful grace. The stench of entrails
a merciful reminder we are observers, not participants.

Bushman Exhibition
(Cape Town, 1996)

On a glossy dais, torso moulds complete
with vaginal slits and semi-erect penises
splay in an arc; their amber opacity
seeming to intensify light, yet draw it in.

For all the absence of faces to betray
embarrassment, such treatment warrants
an unease beyond their being nakedly
on show to both sexes simultaneously.

Plaster limbs and detritus heaped
in a cordoned-off section heighten
the sense of desecration and shame
issuing from their wrinkled presence.

Rather than such spotlit exposure,
this profanation of their privacy
at some trendy curator's whim,
I'd confer a dignified seclusion

in accord with their culture and history:
cave-painters, honey-harvesters;
from the Stone Age to ours, miraculous
survivors in the drought-stricken Kalahari.

Survivor

Slitted against unsteady candlelight
the eyes opposite, for all their laughter-lines,
have been near death. We've been told that.

A wild-life photographer writing a book
he was charged by an old Kruger bull
and trampled unconscious, ribs broken,

a hip dislocated, skin scoured from face
and arms by the bristled foreleg he clung to;
saved somehow from the tusks' *coup de grâce*.

He converses fluently, in measured tones;
listens well. Shows no hint of machismo.
He doesn't need to. He is the real thing.

Later under a hissing paraffin-lamp
we learn that what gnaws at him is why,
having him in its power, the elephant

let him live. Beyond this (real
measure of the man) how it is likely
to react when it next senses his smell.

Jedebe Camp

Trust

Spiky umbels of papyrus bob against my face
as Trust, the head poler, steers through
channels scarcely wide enough to take us.
Reaching an island of baobab, Trust places

a finger to his lips, points at a silhouette
bunched high on a fork: a Pels fishing owl.
I can just pick it out – a blotch of cinammon
and white. Trust gives the thumbs-up.

Poling the mokoro back across the lagoon
he says he hopes his son will go to school
(as he didn't) and learn to read and write
(which his father did, in the diamond mine).

He names the water-birds in his own tongue
and Latin; showing no bitterness
at working, after deductions for food
and board, for a miserly daily rate.

Next day on the plane, I'll find myself seated
behind a lady who 'came all the way from Minnesota
just to see the Pels: worth every cent, believe me':
member of neither a rare nor an endangered species.

Water Two

Our boat moored to the reeds, Water Two
catches three tiger-fish, myself none.
Nor the elderly Zimbabwean in the bow.
Suddenly at 7 a.m., we are into a shoal

of barbel. After three revolutions
my reel screams, then slackens –
the leader bitten through. I land a bream.
The mozzies take over. 'Tiger next time!'

Alongside our catch, on the grass,
instead of the customary fly-box
the size 6 shoe of a former Miss S. Africa
here on a promotional tour. In the small hours

I think of her stretching those lissom limbs;
while in the next tent the Zimbabwean
laments Mugabe's latest sequestrations.
Hourly, the snuffle of hippo

in the surrounding swamp. Already, Okavango
a jewel, in the brain. After coffee and fruit,
I find my backpack speckled with birdshit.
The previous day's catch, fish-eagle bait.

Over the desert

Entering the Kalahari the pure waters
of the Delta, rather than form an estuary,
peter out in a depth of sand so great
even major earth tremors leave no trace

but are absorbed before reaching the surface.
Subjecting our lives, scarcely
more substantial, to varied analogy:
refreshment, or drought, of the spirit;

placing ourselves at others'
disposal; from this, to loss
of enlightenment over the centuries.
Below, a terrain *in extremis*,

dry valleys and fossil dunes
extending to the horizon and beyond;
the world's curve, billions of sandgrains.
Through a blur of condensation

imagine mirage-like, hazy and wavery,
an ancient Bushman and his wife, alone
in the thornveld, awaiting the hyenas
through whom they will join their ancestors.

[1993]

152

VII

Early Days

Connections

Changing trains at Glasgow Central *en route*
for a poetry workshop in Kilmarnock I visit
the bookstall which has, needless to say, none
of my volumes on display. Nor any sign
on the departures board of my connection,
I'm so early. Eventually it appears:
objective reality, at least, restored. Soon
the old litany: Dunlop, Stewarton, Kilmaurs...

As my fellow-travellers, secure in their
identities or otherwise, journey on
towards Sanquhar, Carlisle, my reception
counters expectation: a strummed guitar,
the car in a tarmacked space where rails once were,
set in cobbles, to ease the dray-horses' burden.
To an unaccustomed music, and hyacinths in bloom,
the decades dissolve, and we coast into town.

School motto

Among my memories
a smell of modelling clay
(this before coloured plasticine)

rows of Mickey Mouse
gas-masks (placing me
in the early 40s)

and school caps, regularly
floating like rowan berries
down the Marnock water.

Our infants mistress
Annie C. MacLarty FEIS
took us to her ample bosom

before handing us over
to Davy Gordon, who ruled
with a rod of iron.

In senior school
we were further matured
by two breakdowns and a suicide.

Later our French master
went into mourning, when
a colleague's son got only

a third at Aberdeen.
By then, we others had gone
our own way: unshriven,

but trying (some of us)
to *do justly, love mercy*,
and walk humbly.

New Farm Loch

We skated here after school,
breath visible in the frosty air,
chestnuts sizzling, the ice
ringing. Or played football,

blazers for goals, Tom Campbell
ghosting down the wing,
others less skilled
picked as a cock or a hen.

Drained long since,
the loch's declivity
holds a housing estate.
Yet I sense presences

blowing on their fingers
as if all these years later
my schooldays were pursuing me
through acres of trees

no longer there. The one
tangible reminder a hole
in my left knee, where
the heel of a skate sank in.

Arm's reach

Of moments treasured:
having scaled the tree,
ripe pears gathered
unbruised. Some
peeled and preserved
in syrup. The remainder
each year, painstakingly
stored in paper and straw.
The tubbed windfall, mush
for wasps. These days, even
could I climb to the top,
I'd most likely find
the branch and its fruit
just out of arm's reach.

Mirror image

Evening drawing in, I revisit old
haunts: the Burns monument, smaller
than I recall; St Marnock's, trees squat
as ever; and facing the Dick Institute
the sandstone Academy, dominant on its hill.

Over a couple of pints in the Goldberry
I'm told I don't sound like I'm really
from Killie, the intervening years
having added an overlay. But things seem
to go smoothly. So that by the time

I reach the station I'm confident
I could pass for local. Till reflected
in the waiting-room window, I see
a familiar figure carrying a plastic
bag emblazoned 'Ayrshire and the Burns country'.

Wild Flowers

I didn't know *lupinus polyphyllus* as such, in those days:
simply that our manse garden was rampant with displays
of varying blue; nor that this converging in colour
of massed spikes, year after year, was a reverting to nature.

Oblivious, we lay in their ribbed and scented dens,
bees blundering by, under clouds of chiffon. As intense
were the stained-glass windows we gazed at on Sundays,
the congregation dwindling – successive generations

heading for housing schemes, but still the appeals
for the fabric fund, the carillon of bells;
the burden ever greater, for fewer to bear.
Compare *epilobium angustifolium*, similarly

tall-stemmed, but a looser, fluffier flower,
its mauve spires pointed out by my mother
when we went for runs in the family car, till we'd cry
'Guess what, rosebay willow-herb!' Found mainly

on disused railways, it proliferates where factories were;
reminder of jobs lost, of bitterness and despair.
In abundance, willow-herb and lupin demonstrate
the slow dereliction of Church and State.

Terra Firma

The church of which my father was minister
lowered over my boyhood, its front elevation
imprinted on the retina; an endowed carillon
spendthrift expenditure of a sum more
practical if put towards the maintenance
of rotting roof timbers and friable sandstone.
Although latterly dwarfed by the Police Station
and Sheriff Court opposite, an architectural
survey recently lauded its structure
from hood-moulded main door to battlemented tower,
not to mention *the pulpit's fine expression*
of the crescendo of the Gothic revival...

We'd never have guessed (far less cared)
when as children we fidgeted on hard pews,
that those encompassing walls in future years
would be praised as *scholarly perpendicular* –
a paradox sharpened by the then snobbery
of the town's more class-conscious clergy
one of whom murmured, after his ordination,
'Of course St Marnock's isn't on the map, Conn.'
Throughout his calling, in ways I was then
too young to comprehend, he remained his own man:
voicing concern for single mothers, whom
the Kirk's committees saw as 'fallen women';

and believing an unfashionable ecumenicalism
the way to enlightenment, debating at Coodham
and courting the Kilmarnock Standard's abuse
by counting among his friends, RC priests.
As through a glass darkly, I have come
to a more comprehending admiration
for the industry and integrity
he must have channelled into his ministry –
rather than any inheriting of beliefs: partly
because he never exerted pressure
but permitted me to go my own way,
doubtless praying it would not be to purgatory.

159

Those moments uppermost, at a lifetime's remove,
of austere ritual, redeemed by love
under the lights of the Christmas tree;
and at harvest festivals, ripe sheaves
round the walls of the shadowy vestibule,
fruit heaped before the communion-table,
then the delivery of flowers and vegetables
by the Bible Class: a child's view of the tangible
manifestations of others' belief in Divinity,
not the tenets sustaining it. Today
the building stands, like a preserved dragon –
forbidding still, but no longer breathing flame.

Peace and Plenty

On autumn Saturdays we'd cycle
to Caprington Estate with its great
chestnut trees: the lawns littered,
each spiky bur split on impact,
ripeness preserved intact.

Pockets filled, we hurled up sticks
to dislodge what more we could –
eager to get at the Upper Crust
with their stately homes and shiny
Daimlers, the only way we knew.

Ingrained, a callow awareness
of revolutionary days, eggs thrown
at carriages, aristos done down.
Their ruined mansions seen later
as bombastic parodies of what they were;

our middle-classness an encumbrance
rather than aligning us
with miners' families
or those in the neat cottages
known as Peace and Plenty,

harking back to an age
presaging a New Dawn.
Hard to take, the fruits
of promise not justice
but a polarisation such

as we've seen; retributive
Government seeking scapegoats
among Society's weakest;
stooping to enlist folk-myth
in ways we never dreamt of.

In Your Dreams

(for James Aitchison)

Choosing between Jung and Freud
revealed, I was told, the kind
of father I'd have preferred.
My affinity, I confess, ever
with the twinkling eyed one:
so much that he preoccupied
my waking thoughts for years
(only he could vouch for hours
of sleep). Later I encountered
another from the same mould:
Konrad Lorenz, more mellow
than rigid rules would allow –
and so transposed them
that one night I came across
the analyst up to his waist
in a smooth-flowing stream,
hotly pursued by patients
in the guise of greylag geese.

White Tulips

Over the years, now decades, memories sporadically
surface for no seeming reason: among them one
of a classmate's sister who, playing one day
at the Creamery, must have tripped and fallen in.
I still shudder involuntarily, at the pain
encountered, the scalding of her skin; and can
but pray her engulfing was mercifully speedy.

As I sit in the garden this fragrant May afternoon
she comes to mind, incongruous light-years away.
First there's the shiver that coursed through us,
who at that age thought ourselves scatheless.
Only after this, do I consciously take in
these tulips beside me, their ghostly whiteness
grown suddenly diaphanous in the light breeze.

Norman Collie at Sligachan Inn

*Collie is still up in Skye like an eagle in his eyrie but I hope
he will get tired of that lonely vigil and come back to London.*
F.G. DONNAN, 1939

Ropes and ice-axes stashed, the climbers
troop into the dining-room, nodding towards
the fine-featured octogenarian who slowly
sips his wine. Puffing his pipe afterwards

in the corrugated-iron smoking-room, eyes
like quartz chips, he gives nothing away
at their expressions of amazement that
so many peaks thought previously unclimbed

should be capped by such similar cairns.
He smiles as they plan the next day's
routes and traverses; recalling his own
and Mackenzie's mastery of the Bhasteir Tooth,

solving the massive shadow of the Cioch...
They say goodnight, oblivious of his
unspoken benediction: 'Set your sights
on your aspirations' limit. The summit won,

let the eye gaze, the spirit brim. Then
the gods of the mountain not taking kindly
to abuse of hospitality, make your way down,
recharged and calm. Nearing the treeline

you will encounter colours intense as any
you recall, cow-bells resonant in the inner ear.
Gaze back at the crest where you've been,
its blueness nothing on its own – rather

the use you put it to'. Continents merge
as he drifts towards sleep, pursued by troupes
of Edwardian ladies, ropes round hourglass waists,
who slip from precipices, abseil into the abyss.

Later he turns in a cold sweat: Mummery
and Whymper, as on a glass plate, spin past
in a neon blaze; voices in whispers ask,
was the rope frayed or mysteriously cut?

Until eased by a chuckle, at his request
that Leverhulme sponsor an attempt on Everest:
in return, they'd plant a flag on the summit,
a bar of Sunlight Soap emblazoned on it.

Air and Water

for James Rankin

The Bible beaten into him (thrashed excessively
but exclusively on week-days, to preserve the calm
of the Sabbath) Muir one of three children (the others
left with their mother in Dunbar) taken to settle
in the Wisconsin prairie. First Fountain Lake;

then Hickory Hill where when he was twelve his father,
desperate to hit water, lowered him in a bucket
with hammer and chisel, to hack obdurate sandstone out.
Eighty feet down, the air so carbonised he collapsed
and could have died, if not hauled to the surface.

Subsequently University, and departure from home:
thereafter his own man. But nightmares the remainder
of his life, choking in an underground pit – the father
stentorian as ever; his comeuppance that his son,
Nature's disciple, would not credit its glories to God.

Years later on the Yosemite trail, the thrawn
old Scotchman he'd become leaping from a snow-pool
to challenge his President to a wrestling-bout:
an immigrant, battling for his American dream,
tackling Big Business head-on. The marvel, he won.

Roosevelt, needing the Californian vote, later
to welch on him, turning Hetch-Hetchy into a dam.
Muir still worshipping his open spaces, the supreme
escape from that father who drove him below ground.
What better than a Wilderness, to liberate the mind.

The Ocean of Time

(i.m. George Mackay Brown)

I

Hard to think your one-man
welcoming party has gone;
your prow-chin left
harbour, its voyage done;

your workroom window
facing out to sea
once a source of light,
now a blind eye;

no handwritten note
pinned to your door
saying you'll be
back shortly.

The iron harpoon
you were given in the Year
of the Whale has found
a good home with Erlend.

II

More and more your
friends miss you; this
the first winter
they'll be without you.

Yet your presence
all pervasive:
in Tam's book-cave,
Gunnie's magic lens;

night-tread from Hopedale,
scratch of pen, salt
at the pane; word-geese
massed on the skyline.

And as the mists clear,
a familiar figure
seen wraithlike
on headland and shore.

III

Everyone's talk
so warming
it's a shame
you can't join them.

Or simply
rock slowly
in your old chair,
Gypsy on your knee.

Rain blatters
the window;
dark shapes
claw at the pane.

Over Hamnavoe,
a double rainbow:
vision and dream,
a perfect cradling.

IV

South of Yesnaby
a solitary seal-pup
seems stranded
far from the ebb.

It belly-flaps
over the rocks,
ungainly till
it plunges

and reappears
riding the crest,
eyeing me from safety,
all muscular sheen.

Your life spent
in *your* element,
a dogged defiance
of surging forces.

    V

Weaver of tales,
a spirit to match,
you caught the feel
of these Islands

merging emblem
and meaning, welding
'holy and carnal
in one flame'.

Fitting, in the hush
of St Magnus,
to come across lines
from your poems

in the key
to the west window:
'golden sun, wheat-
stalks, fishes'.

    VI

I see you on a blue
bench by the pier
against a white wall,
all fisherknit jersey

and tangled hair,
eager as a boy
going to sea
for the first time.

Now in the long-ship
of the setting sun
your last journey.
Gannet and gull

on the cliff-edge squall,
as the fiery vessel
glides behind Hoy.
Darkness. A muffled bell.

Stolen Light

A shiver crosses Loch Stenness
as of thousands of daddy-long-legs
skittering on the surface.
In total stillness
thunderheads close in.

Lead-shot from a blunderbuss
the first flurries come.
The elements have their say;
the depths riven
as by some monster.

The impulse to run
hell-for-leather
lest this a prelude
to one of the Great Stones
clumping to the water.

A friend is writing
a book on poetry
and inspiration.
Brave man – imagine him
in flippers and wet-suit

poised on the edge:
a charging of nerve-ends
too rapid to track,
or underwater treasure
you hold your breath and dive for?

First Light

Near Nunnerie, where Daer and Potrail meet,
highstepping it through early morning mist:
a troupe of llamas; one brown, four white,
their head-erect posture midway between
goat and camel, last thing we dreamt we'd see.

Approaching the bank, they stop in unison
and stand motionless, maybe in contemplation
of their near perfect reflections, or simply
for a good nostrilful of us, then move on;
all but the largest, who gazes quizzically

as if asking, 'Do you suspect we exist
only as some mutation of the spirit
of the place? Have it as you please.'
Then dismissing philosophical fripperies
he turns and splashes through a hoop of light.

Presence
(i.m. Deirdre Keaney)

Each time I come fishing here now brings me past
where you hit what fate had brought the other way.
Tonight, the April light fading, the ripples flatly

slapping the bow assume an added melancholy. But as
the dazzling intricacies of even a minute ago
give way to darkness, and the hills enclosing us

become undulations of velvet (as Border hills do),
so in a manner no less real because wondrous
you seem both present, and absent, in the afterglow.

Return to Provence

Odd to find ourselves zigzagging
round fields of lavender as we did last time
seeking shelter from the rain.
See those swallow-tails, the air steeped in resin?

The harder we scour new horizons, the more
familiar the lie of the land. We slow down
not because the race is run, but for fear
we may catch up with who we once were.

Will we some day find the pines gone,
wells poisoned, no creatures near –
and wonder at what stage the change began?
Even if only in the imagination

light as pigeon-wings, by way
of a last gift, may our lips touch fleetingly.

Jawbone Walk

'It must have been all underwater
once. You're welcome to share my bench.
Where was I? Yes, a time when the entire

Meadows roared with the surge of seas.
Could you spare something towards lunch?
Thank you, sir. Yes, rather than trees

soughing, translucent waves rampaging. How else
do you imagine that arch got there? The ocean
has *haves* and *have-nots* too, you know, though

you might not think it. Never hear
of the scavenger crab? Don't suppose you
give it a thought. Must've been millions

of years before the Brontosauruses
came huffing this way, far less the Legions
who tramped north, only to disappear.

Much appreciated miss, no need to scurry away...
In the Pleistocene Age or thereabouts,
it must have been. Excuse me sir, have you the price

of a cup of tea? That's rich, I must say –
you wouldn't like to add a sandwich? Yes,
those jaw-bones have been around a long time.'

As he pockets my sub, and keen to remain
a one-off do-gooder, not form a habit,
I ask can we treat it as a season ticket.

Past bedraggled Sunday footballers,
kite-fliers and frisbee-throwers,
dogs single-mindedly at their business,

he heads down Middle Meadow Walk towards
the Infirmary outbuildings:
yellow-eyed, looming Mastodons.

Inheritance

When first we came to this city
there were nights we would lie
too tense to sleep for fear
the noises we could hear,

muffled blows, a woman's screams,
stemmed from real violence.
So it proved. In the small hours
she rang our bell, in her nightdress,

weals on her face, to use the phone.
One morning to our relief, they'd gone.
More pleasing sounds, if rarer silences,
now infiltrate our living space.

For all that, this a land ill at ease
with itself. Brutality decrees
its own choreography: small children
fastened at the wrist by coloured ribbon;

pavements laden with flowers
in cellophane. The fascination
of lens and screen forcing us
to choose, or not, to be voyeurs.

Short, from tempering justice
to compounding bestiality.
As deep, fear of being rendered,
through familiarity, immune to horror.

So are we at the mercy of the world we live in,
yet blessed as to some: one's son on heroin;
another traced to London, not heard of again.
The test, more and more, just to endure.

If so, what the likely adequacy
of our strain? Dawn comes. Reluctantly
I open the shutters, turn the radio on.
Scientists have found a link in human evolution:

a fossilised skeleton, adding to our ancestry
a further million years. What family-tree
can compete with primordial gloom, the cave-man
in you croaks sagely, to the cave-man in me.

At the Reservoir

As I skirt Thriepmuir a car door opens
and a voice asks where I'm heading. The water's
edge seemingly a farm boundary, I prepare
to retrace my steps – but garb and demeanour
flouting no convention, am permitted to walk on.

A quaffing at a pure source: geese ready
to head north; permutations of umber
and green. So that when a moorhen scutters
from under my feet, and a bunting in mufti
nose-dives into a reed-bed and sways there

like a vaulter on a pole, I contain
a spontaneous chortle: just not done,
to distract attention from the mundane
business of householder and family-man
or old age, our fast-approaching destination.

Losing Touch

I *Losing touch*

I feel so confused. If only
I could sleep peacefully away.
We are living far too long nowadays.
Still, ninety is a good age, you agree?

Like a mantra, over and over,
between journeyings to far-off
resorts; exotic countries
and residences, vicariously

visited down the years;
now subterfuge experiences.
I envisage her fears
as so many furred moths

in a ferment between her
and the light; a journey
through a trance-like forest,
the abyss so close...

day-to-day life an instrument
she has all but forgotten
how to play – so long in a dusty
loft, its strings slack anyway.

II *Ghosts*

Driving home for Sunday tea, we used
to pass along the highways and byways
of her girlhood, while she reminisced
about school and university days;

pointing out where she caught
the Dalkeith bus, when she taught;
then on our return, Gladstone
Terrace where she was born.

Recalling her graduation ceremony
in the McEwan Hall, the principle's
felicitous 'It seems no one, Mr Liddell,
can pass you, but for the examiners ...'.

Hard not to suspect, afterwards,
I was inheriting her ghosts:
the Meadows swirling with mist,
frilled shapes under the trees

and right where she said they were,
to no skirl of pipes and drums
or male voices in full song,
the Dandy Ninth, going off to War.

III *Vantage point*

I seem hopelessly lost.
Worse than ever. I used
to be in a halfway house.
Nothing approaching this ...

Hardly a stone's throw
from the window, snow
powders Blackford Hill
where she played as a girl.

Little more merciless
than the ageing process:
ice filling the veins;
a hawk's glinting talons.

Her wrist frail on mine
I think despairingly of Man
and his Creator, exploding
from the Sistine ceiling;

yet when helplessly
she beseeches to be gone,
find I can pray only
that *her* will be done.

IV *Oratorio*

She has shown no response
to Holy Week, as in earlier
days and down the years.
Nor do the signatures

on the Easter cards heaped
by her bedside convey other
than that they too relate
to an impenetrable past.

Bach at his most sublime
depicts Death, seen
through Satan vanquished
and Christ risen, as no more

than a gentle slumber
prior to entering Heaven.
The vision of her bowed
head, nodding slowly,

accentuates the mortality
invested in that fragile
frame. The chorus nears
its end. Jubilant voices soar.

At some point during a storm-tossed night
I peer at the faintly luminous face
by my bed, try to calculate
where you might be. At eight-thirty
in the evening, you could well be out

for dinner with Angela and George:
a gathering too discreet to gorge
yourselves American-style, but capable
I'm sure of eating well. Sleep calls.
Bon appetit! I'll let you pay the bill.

*

Two midnights later. You will have flown
(if on schedule) over Hawaii, and soon
be crossing the International date-line:
short-cutting from yesterday to tomorrow.
As I stand at your plant-strewn kitchen window

my heart tells me there should be some sign
visible at least over your own tended garden.
No shooting-star – did I really expect one –
but in the gap between the tenements opposite,
the sky is decked with garlands of pure white.

*

Sunday. I wonder if you're worshipping
in the same neat church I sat in, when
so briefly there. Nothing Victorian,
but stripped pine, with modern carving.
A well-behaved New Plymouth congregation

sang rousingly, then gave the lengthy sermon
full attention – never wavering
(that I could see) as a line of ants came in
one window, skirted the organ screen
and on reaching the far wall, disappeared.

*

Since it is mellow afternoon with you,
treat this short section as a *billet doux*.
I picture you anchored in a bay of blue
where you enjoy, with John and Liffey,
a swim in water (why not the old cliché)

still crystal-clear. Laughter reaches me,
like tinkling bells. From the boat's side
come lappings of applause, as if on cue.
I send my love as, colourfully clad,
carefree you set, then light, your barbecue.

*

Your papyrus plant, which I was to water
on alternate days, forgotten utterly.
The extent of my neglect: its slender
stems are bowed; dried leaftips shrivel;
its elegant parasols, all forlorn.

For such mishaps, desperate remedies. I pour
bottlefuls in, night and morning. No sign
of recovery. Too late the familiar, bitter
lesson: little use a surfeit of affection,
once the initial damage has been done.

*

Your spirit meantime flits about the place,
from those items bought in auctions
in our early days, to the cushions
scattered in the sitting-room, the rummers
and yellow plates displayed downstairs;

elsewhere the angling of a lampshade,
consistent with where the pictures
look their best. And latest of all,
your newly-lined bedspread: untenanted
it keenly awaits you, discreetly autumnal.

*

And see, against the net curtains
like a screen print: the papyrus
in its brass bowl. Assiduously
cared for since my sin of omission,
it has recovered miraculously –

conjuring up visions of Nefertiti,
Thales proclaiming *water is all*;
the rushes Moses was left in,
by the Nile. Yet how convince
you I've hand-maidened it well?

*

What about: only yesterday I cut
its largest leaves into strips;
the pith beaten, and rolled
with mud substitute; then pressed
under the mattress on wooden slats

with fitting devotions, to produce
the flimsy parchment this is written on.
Forgive its clumsy hieroglyphs. Even
if you don't believe a word of them,
the important thing is: welcome home.

Museum Piece

Through swing-doors, down stone stairs,
   along corridors crammed with items
   not on display: furred crates, shrouded
   warriors, glinting models of sailing vessels,
   curled pennant to bowsprit pure silver

to emerge with a painting I'd had framed
   (no need to spool thread, because steered
   by a pallid guide with a security chit)
   to the glare, who'd think of it, of Glasgow sunlight.

Kelvingrove half a lifetime away
   I still marvel (how our lives founder,
   heads bobbing in time's flotsam)
   at those galleons...sumptuous, subterranean.

Carnyx

Priest-mask, pig-snorkel, prow-peak
   glinting in its glass case? Chess-piece
   crafted for Cúchulainn; fossil sea-horse
   surfaced from centuries in peat-juice?

Treasure more mysterious: a boar's-head
   wrought in bronze; mastery of palate
   and sprung wooden tongue passed down
   in secrecy, Pictish father to son.

Such raucous resonance, from so slender
   a column of air, as struck terror
   into invaders. Fit too to proclaim,
   given occasion, a Nation's resurgence.

Te Maori

Plane-loads of numbered wooden crates
delivered to the Metropolitan Museum
for the *Te Maori* Exhibition, a run
of near-disasters is ascribed to those
whose spirits they contain signalling anger
at being regarded as mere *objets d'art*.

After discussion behind the scenes,
the opening ceremony goes smoothly.
Then the discovery of severe notching
in a jade head coincides with dispute
over an extension of dates: the matter
resolved, damage no longer seen.

Where, given our ingrained materialism –
the absence of green-stone carvings
on our lawns, combs cut from bone –
might the spirits of our ancestors
reside? Up to us, to preserve
our own repositories of intuition.

Outlook

I study my hands
on the keyboard,

lined and bent
as age takes its toll:

no flames flicker
at these fingertips.

Yet seated
in your garden,

not idling but
seeking "inspiration",

see bursting
from the gnarled

buddleia branches
not just blooms

but (this a crazy
year for butterflies)

emergent clouds
of Painted Ladies.

Letters to Iain

(for Iain Crichton Smith)

I

Dear Iain – nothing written
for months, now a sudden
inundation in response
to your illness, a blur
of hope and trepidation
in the face of despair.

*

How speak of *death* and *dying*
in your presence – surely
there must always be hope?

True to yourself and others
your courage lets the subject
be broached. From the bright

crevasses of your mind,
prising words like jewels
from the air, warriors emerge

each braver than the one
before...sooner or later
to return on his shield.

*

I keep seeing two helmeted figures:
one in the throes of illness;
the other his joyous likeness
cavorting in space, like spun glass.

*

You saw the *dark companion* as 'the real poem
alongside the actually created one'. On my way
to visit you, a doppel-ganger in the train window
becomes a ghostly imprint, against moor and sky.
And I think of the circling fins of those other
dark companions you have overcome. Now the worst
wants to lock you in his foul, black armour.

*

Above all, may a miracle
yet happen:

a white, not a black sail
appear over the horizon.

II

One of the men in your ward
has his TV on: a big race from France;
at Ibrox a game is about to begin.

You turn drowsily, the still centre
of your universe. The horses come under
starter's orders, the rabid crowds roar.

*

Then Donalda arrives
and your world changes.
She is gentle, yet strong:
so strong I'm sure she
could bend bars of iron.

If she could have her way
there would be no illness,
no fear. No endless journeys,
no wondering when
you will be home again.

She sits calmly,
her eyes on you,
your hand in hers.
If anyone can make
a miracle happen, she will.

*

And everywhere the nurses
robust and rumbustious

plastic bibs like fishtails
who bathe and feed you.

Now jocular now cajoling,
they circumscribe your world.

I wonder how they seem
to you, those Kindly Ones.

*

The last time we saw you
was at home in Taynuilt:
you smiled and quizzed us.
Now it is as though
something had left you,
rendered you defenceless.
On the polished floor
your slippers could be
highlit by Vermeer.

*

Your Argyll slopes
are tawny flanks
flecked with light,
the trees turning.

You don't have these
in your strange room:
just those horses,
the crowds baying.

May you soon be home,
continuing the fight
among benign mountains,
icy Etive sparkling.

III

Thanks to you we see
things differently, more acutely;
love detectable, where
we never thought to look.

On the cover of your new book
Tutankhamun from a golden throne
gazes at his queen – she at him:
a radiance spanning the ages,
through the artist's vision and your own.

Just out is a study
not of the divine king
so much as the manner of his death:
x-rays showing blows to the skull.

Your distinction lies
in transcending these;
tenderness preserved
at whatever price:

an audacious capturing of human trembling.

IV

The phone rings: the news
we have been dreading.
'Iain died at twenty
to five this morning.'

Mercifully to the end
the interchange of love
through touch, and glance.
Superseded by peace.

*

I think of whatever
is Gaelic for *sea-birds*
winging you home,
your singing done.

Death's Corrievracken
flexing its muscles
just long enough
to let you through.

*

Today I walk in the Botanics,
simply to think about you, away
from the ringing phone. Behind
each tree-trunk, an invisible

version of you; playing a game
of hide-and-seek it seems, until
the whistles blow and the keepers
start shouting 'Closing time'.

*

Your voice on radio
as if you were in the room,
so natural, no hint
of what was to come.

In the old days
the wireless used
to crackle like dry
leaves on the line.

I imagine them falling,
containing your shape,
until the breeze
breathes them to nothing.

The programme ends
with your favourite song
about the white swan.
Autumn fully your season.

*

I watch as a swan, its wings
smirched by black stains,
tries to preen itself clean.

So words like *death* and *dead*
tarnish you: how subdue them?
From somewhere – the far shore

or a recess of the mind –
comes gliding, neck erect,
all hauteur and grace,

a swan of burnished ebony.